From Performance to Praise

Moving Music Ministry to the Next Level

Joe Pace

"Joe Pace is a remarkable instructor. His insights into the areas of worship and music ministry are a must for anyone struggling to move beyond the realm of performance into the courts of praise."

- Michael Coleman
President/CEO
Integrity Media

From Performance to Praise
ISBN 0-9712701-8-X
Copyright © 2004 by Joseph W. Pace II
Cover Design: LaTanya Terry, LTerry Designs

Published by Serenity Publishing & Communications, Inc.
P.O. Box 282282
Nashville, TN 37228

Printed in the United States of America.

TABLE OF CONTENTS

INTRODUCTION

This book is for pastors, musicians, ministers of music, choir directors, choir members, praise team members, sound personnel, and anyone else who has a hand in or is aspiring to become involved with executing music ministry either within a local congregation or professional industry setting.

Between each of these pages is a part of my heart. My personal experiences, let downs, disappointments, mistakes, triumphs, and victories have been poured out in this book. During my years within the music ministry and industry, I have seen the frustrations of pastors and music ministers wanting desperately to move their worship experiences to another level. I've seen abuses of the music ministry and those who have been tremendous stewards of their gifts. I've looked into the eyes of star-struck musicians and singers yearning to perform, and I've watched 70-year old mothers proud to just play the piano through devotional service. I've seen things that have worked well in music ministry and things that definitely have not. Each has influenced me tremendously.

However, as I live I understand daily that we <u>each</u> have a unique part to play in the larger scheme of life. As God's plans unfold before us and through us, there must be a greater sensitivity to Him and His heart in all matters. Things are not always as they seem or as we necessarily think they should be. The same is true for music ministry, and I hope that something you read and receive from these pages acts as the pendulum that begins to turn your view of music ministry around. Affecting your execution of this priestly call is my ultimate goal, and for that, I make no apologies. I genuinely want to see all of us raise our level of ministry and excellence. We owe it to ourselves to give the Father all He requires from us. He has set the stage so that we are indeed the real benefactor of the sincere praise and worship we give to Him.

I want to address the title of this book—*From Perfor-*

mance to Praise for a moment. Let me be clear that this title is not meant to indicate that there is anything inherently wrong with performance. According to Webster's Dictionary, performance is simply defined as *"the act of performing (doing) a deed or feat; a formal exhibition or presentation."* The title is intended, however, to bring attention to and provoke thought about the tendency in music ministries and certainly within the music industry to sometimes inordinately focus on performance rather than His presence; individual showmanship rather than the vertical relationship; entertaining rather than engaging; style rather than substance; and spirited music rather than spiritual music. I could go on and on.

Performance has its place because technical excellence, the perfecting of your gift, and presentation are essential. We will discuss all of that in this book. However, if you get nothing else out of this book, please understand that the foundation for everything we do in music ministry is based upon the Father and our relationship with Him. It's not about your choreography; it's about your connection. It's not about your flair, skill, or musicianship; it's about your faithfulness to your relationship with God. No Real Relationship—No Real Worship.

Perhaps you feel that there is no hope for change or a fresh visitation from the Holy Spirit within your particular congregation, or maybe you feel as though it is time for you to leave the choir or team because you feel unappreciated by people. Before you sign off from the music ministry for good, I invite you to come inside the world of music ministry from a practical, yet challenging standpoint. This is not a novel with which you should snuggle under a comfortable blanket to read for pleasure. This book is for those who are tired of the unspoken things being hidden and the same old song being sung with the same stale excuse being given for mediocrity.

I have been given the mandate of challenge and encouragement. As you read, I warn you that you may see yourself as well as others, but the goal is for you to correct the things that you can identify within yourself and pray for change in others. I promise you if you do this, a new anointing and grace for service will come upon you and undoubtedly cause you to be an agent of change not only in your local congregation and music ministry, but also in your life of love and service to the Father.

You are about to discover why you do what you do in music, what significance it has in the overall scheme of things, and how your music ministry can progress from just dutiful performance to dynamic praise.

-Joe Pace

1

In The Beginning..

As we look into the concept of music ministry, there are a variety of places we can begin. The subject of music ministry is as vast as any other area of ministry or vein of teaching. As you read this book, it will take you along a systemic path of growth and revelation in order to make your role in the area of music ministry more effective, purposeful, and enjoyable. Therefore, the question is: Where do we start? The answer is simple. We start at the beginning.

"In the beginning God created..."(Genesis 1:1). We can agree that God was the Creator of everything. Many scriptures point to that fact (Hebrews 1:10, Psalms 102:25). There is no way to refute that God Himself has fashioned and created the essence of every aspect of life as we know it. Everything we see today has been formed or developed from what God has given to us.

The same is true for music. To look at music in its purest form, we see the beauty and power of a tool. Yes, a tool. It was a tool given not initially to man, but to an angel to glorify God in heaven. Music was and is the component that created and maintained an atmosphere of worship in heaven. Music is still going on in heaven today, but there has been a corporate restructuring. A hostile take over was brewing, and it caused the very first high profile scandal. The headlines read: HE'S OUTTA HERE: CHIEF MUSICIAN OUSTED!

To many this would seem funny, but it's really quite sad. When we read the scriptures that describe the vast beauty, wisdom, and effectiveness of this angel (Lucifer), it is mind boggling that who and what he was ended up not being enough for him. There are things said about him that have never been recorded about anyone else in scripture.

"Son of man, take up a lamentation upon the king of Tyrus, and say unto him, Thus saith the Lord God; Thou sealest up the sum, full of wisdom, and perfect in beauty. Thou hast been in Eden the garden of God; every precious stone was thy covering, the sardius, topaz, and the diamond, the beryl, the onyx, and the jasper, the sapphire, the emerald, the carbuncle, and gold: the workmanship of thy tabrets and thy pipes was prepared in thee in the day that thou was created."

(Ezekiel 28:12-13)

Can you imagine your body being covered with precious gems and stones? Your value is without measure, and you are indeed the most beautiful creature in your circle. Your purpose is to lead, and your position is one of great esteem. You don't need to climb up the corporate ladder because you were created to head your department! What a thought! But this was not enough for Lucifer; he wanted more. He wanted it all—he wanted to be God, and there were consequences for those short-circuited thoughts.

"....I beheld Satan as lightning fall from heaven."

(Luke 10:18)

"How art thou fallen from heaven, O Lucifer, son of the morning! How art thou cut down to the ground, which didst weaken the nations!"

(Isaiah 14:12)

When this unprecedented event took place, what did the scene look like? What was the daily operational model before 'The Fall'? What is happening right now? What were the job descriptions? Let's look at who was doing what.

"In the year that king Uzziah died I saw also the Lord sitting upon a throne, high and lifted up, and his train filled the temple. Above it stood the seraphims: each one had six wings; with twain he covered his face, and with twain he covered his feet, and with twain he did fly. And one cried unto another, and said, Holy, holy, holy, is the Lord of hosts: the whole earth is full of his glory. And the posts of the door moved at the voice of him that cried, and the house was filled with smoke."

(Isaiah 6:1-4)

Isaiah shows us that worship is ongoing. It did not cease when Lucifer was banished from heaven; it continues every second of every day as we know it, and rest assured, it will continue for eternity. There has never been and will never be a time that praise and worship will cease.

John gives us a very similar account of the activity of the angels in heaven. They were created to praise and worship God the Father. The job description of the angels—all angels—is to give honor and praise to God. That will NEVER change.

"And I beheld, and I heard the voice of many angels round about the throne and the beasts and the elders: and the number of them was ten thousand times ten thousand, and thousands of thousands; Saying with a loud voice, Worthy is the Lamb that was slain to receive power, and riches, and wisdom, and strength, and honor, and glory, and blessing."

(Rev. 5:11,12)

This host of angels was the group God created Lucifer to lead. He was the minister of music, choir director, musician, and sound person all wrapped into one. Every instrument that was needed to create the perfect pitch for the perfect note was made inside of his body. If the angels needed a little bass to give the perfect praise to God, then he needed only to call that out of himself. His name, Lucifer, means "Day Star." He was also called "Anointed Cherub" and "Son of the Morning." What majestic depictions of what his function was at the throne of God.

> *Music was and is the component that created and maintained an atmosphere of worship in heaven.*

However, the very anointing to lead the angelic host in worship turned him into an outlaw. No longer able to fulfill the core of his calling to the Father. He could no longer lead anyone or anything into the presence of God. He became the archenemy of pure worship, or worship that is holy, majestic, perfect, and in pure harmony with the heart of God. He is a rebel with a purpose that no longer leads *to*, but *away from*, God.

It is important to remind all people who say they are called to any aspect of the music ministry to recognize that they are functioning in a capacity that is well-known to their adversary. He is no longer known as "Day Star"; his name has been changed to Satan. He has been stripped of his purpose, and there is no glory to be given him. Yes, he still leads angels, but they have a new mission because of their new assignment. And, I would dare say, they have a great interest in those of us who not only dare to stand in the shoes that he filled, but also the shoes he stood in better than anyone else created. Every sound we make reminds him of what he lost.

This assault should not come as a surprise because, from a very practical stance, people tend to have a degree of cynicism toward someone that functions in their place after they have been terminated—especially when they no longer have the authority that came along with the position. For example, human nature dictates that if a person is fired from a job that he or she spent most of his or her time functioning in quite effectively, he or she has some level of animosity towards his or her replacement because something they had was given to someone else.

There has never been and will never be a time that praise and worship will cease.

The point here is to know the history of your opponent enough to understand the dynamics of the spiritual playing field. The more you know about the aspects of your calling, the easier it will be for you to identify changes that you need to make when assessing the facilitation of growth in the music ministry of which you are a part.

Next, let's look at the characteristics Lucifer demonstrated in order to turn a platform of perfect praise and worship into a mockery of music that has attempted to invade music ministries today.

2

Check Yourself!

There is no doubt that we can see Satan's influence throughout secular music. The more vile, seductive, violent, and sadistic the music, the more recognition, accolades, and monetary gain it seems to generate. Satan has attempted to set a pattern of behavioral precedent for anyone involved in music. As Christians, we take issue with the thought that Satan could be influencing our musical foundations, and we should. However, let us stop and take a closer look at the pattern that was attempted to be established in heaven, yet has ultimately taken root and grown rapidly on earth. The reason Lucifer had to be evicted had nothing to do with his ability, splendor, or effectiveness and everything to do with the motivation of his heart.

As we highlight the behavioral pattern that caused the disenchantment of musical perfection, consider your surroundings. Do you see any of these elements present in the music ministry in which you are involved? Can you identify changes that need to be made? And, more importantly, do you see traces of these characteristics in you?

"You, the bright morning star, have fallen from the sky. You brought down other nations. Now you are brought down. You said to yourself, 'I'll climb to the heaven and place my throne above the highest stars. I'll sit there with the gods far away in the north. I'll be above the clouds, just like God Most High.'"

(Isaiah 14: 12-14 CEV)

"...You were in Eden, the garden of God; every precious stone adorned you: ruby, topaz and emerald, chrysolite, onyx and jasper, sapphire, turquoise and beryl. Your settings and mountings were made of gold; on the day you were created they were prepared. You were anointed as a guardian cherub, for so I ordained you. You were on the holy mount of God; you walked among the fiery stones."   *(Ezekiel 28: 12-14 NIV)*

15

Losing Focus: The Beginning of the End

If there is one question that rings like a wind chime in the hearts of humanity; Christians and non-Christians, it is what are we doing here? What is our purpose? Many attempt to answer this question to no avail, and others never try at all. They just float through life aimlessly as if they have given up the quest to find the answer. But know this. We must answer this question in its most basic form before we can effectively guard ourselves against spiritual destruction in the area of ministry, or, more specifically in this case, music ministry.

Sadly enough, the aforementioned scriptures give us some indication that Lucifer was well aware of the purpose he served in heaven. It was very clear to him that he had stature and ability unique to him. He was not blind; he could see that his being was spectacular and that he shone like a bright light because of the precious stones and gems in him. And there lies the beginning of the end. He looked at himself too long and too intently. Simply put, he took his focus off of worshipping God, which was the answer to his question...why am I here?

The moment we lose our focus or fail to understand why we are singing in the choir, selecting songs, attending rehearsals, tuning our instruments, or adjusting the sound marks the beginning of our end. The primary reason for being involved in music ministry should ultimately be about God the Father. When that is no longer the reason for being, guess what? That is when our worship of God ceases to exist.

"I am the Lord: that is my name: and my glory will I not give to another, neither my praise to graven images."

(Isaiah 42:8)

"Thus saith the Lord the King of Israel, and his redeemer the Lord of hosts; I am the first, and I am the last; and beside me there is no God."

(Isaiah 44:6)

When we focus, we concentrate on something. As participants in music ministry, our primary concentration should be on praising and worshipping God and pleasing Him with pure worship from a sincere heart. That, my friends, can be done by beating two sticks together. The sound is important, but what makes that sound acceptable to God? The direction in which that the sound is being sent—to Him! Anything else is just noise.

"Take thou away from me the noise of thy songs; for I will not hear the melody of thy viols."   *(Amos 5:23)*

We are always focused on something. If you stop and think for a moment, you will realize that your actions have a specific focus before, during, and after you do them. There is never a time that your focus is not on something or someone. Right now, you are focused on reading this book. When you put this book down, your focus or attention will be given to something or someone else.

Lucifer was given only one focus as his reason for being; he was designed and created for one purpose—worship. His focus should have been only to lead the angels into musical melodies and expressions of adoration toward God the Father, but when he observed the response he was getting from the other angels and how receptive God was to the effectiveness of his abilities, he shifted his focus. Instead of looking outside of himself at the glory of God, he began looking inside of himself at his perceived greatness.

*"And you said in your heart, **I will** ascend to Heaven; **I will** exalt my throne above the stars of God; **I will** sit upon the mount of assembly in the uttermost north; **I will** ascend above the heights of the clouds, **I will** make myself like the Most High."*

(Isaiah 14:13,14)

After his focus shifted, everything that was placed in him to give to God was turned upon himself. He turned his gift to exalt God on himself. Since he was pre-programmed only to worship God, he had no choice but to view himself as a god for his gift to be effective. So when we see *I will,* we see his attempts to duplicate the aspects of God on a physical level.

> The primary reason for being involved in music ministry should ultimately be about God the Father.

How does this pertain to your role in the music ministry? The moment you begin to take the focus off God, you too, will turn the same desire to exalt God toward yourself. You might say, "No. I would never do such a thing." Well, that might be true, but have you ever thought to yourself, "I can do this better. If I had my own choir or my own group, it would be much more successful than this?"

This disease commonly begins with the superb ability to exalt something or someone else. Yet, once this gift is turned inwardly, or in this case, goes into remission (to lessen the intensity or seriousness) towards God when it does appear again, the focus has spread to oneself and has begun to metastasize (to spread from an original site to another). It usually comes back more forcefully toward the new origin (self) than it was toward God.

Now we must look further at the dynamics of the new condition. It shows up with one main identifier—the word "I."

Prideful Personnel

"And you said in your heart, I will ascend to Heaven; I will exalt my throne above the stars of God; I will sit upon the mount of assembly in the uttermost north; I will ascend above the heights of the clouds, I will make myself like the Most High."

(Isaiah 14:13,14)

Lucifer did the unthinkable. He was tossed out from his position in heaven at the throne of God. It is important to note that he still has access to the same place out of which he was thrown (See Job 1: 6,7). As people designated to be involved in the music ministry, this indicates that it is more severe to be thrown out of our position with God than to lose our ability to come with others into His presence.

God encourages all of creation to praise and worship Him. That is not designated for the few. As a matter or fact, if mankind does not offer praise unto God, the atmosphere and nature will step into position and exalt Him because of His goodness. So, whenever we cease to offer praise and worship, there are understudies ready to take our place. Who knows what your replacement is—it might just be a rock (Luke 19:40).

When people are downsized out of their positions, there are some things that take place prior to their elimination. God is always looking for progression, so if you are taken out of a position, you must first identify the reason for the shift. You must ask the question, is God moving me up or out? In this scenario concerning Lucifer that we have been dissecting, it is obvious that he was being moved out. Once he took his focus off God, God knew the natural progression was for Lucifer to place his focus on himself. A seed was sown immediately; its name is pride.

"Pride goes before destruction, a haughty spirit before a fall."
(Proverbs 16:18 NIV)

Pride is a word that can offer a dichotomy in its meaning because it has both a positive and negative connotation. On the positive side, pride is "a proper sense of one's dignity or value; self-respect." There is nothing wrong with having a sense of value. In fact, it is healthy to view yourself as a wonderful creation. After all, God has formed you and fashioned you into His image. You are designed in His likeness. You are His master design, intelligent, and full of greatness.

"I will praise You, for I am fearfully and wonderfully made; Marvelous are Your works; And that my soul knows very well."
(Psalms 139:14 NKJV)

Notice in this verse, the first thing David says is, "I will praise You." He identifies his understanding of how unique and wonderful he is as a creation of God, but, he does not separate himself from the adoration of the One that created him. *"And that my soul knows very well."* He affirms that the seat of his emotions and intellect are settled in the fact that *"It is He who has made us and not we ourselves"* (Psalms 100:3). He ensures that praise is on his lips and that his heart is positioned sincerely and reverently toward the Father. What a tremendous model of worship!

On the negative side, pride is defined as "arrogance or conceit; To indulge (oneself) in a feeling of satisfaction." Notice that the flip side of pride is focused on self. The "I" factor. This is the pride that developed in Lucifer's heart and is the offspring of a misplaced focus of worship from God the Father towards himself.

This is no small matter from a music ministry point of view because there are other elements that can foster and even stimulate the growth of a prideful heart if we are not careful. In Proverbs 16:18, the word *haughty* is translated as *'gâbôahh'* in Hebrew, which means *fully arrogant, elevated, exceedingly proud, or haughty.*

> *God encourages all of creation to praise and worship Him.*

Some of the other elements that deserve our attention are things like vanity, accolades, esteem, applause, and power. We will discuss them in greater detail in further chapters, but it bears mentioning that the response people give you must be tempered by you. It was Lucifer's responsibility to continue to exalt God. It was part of his job description to guard himself against pride. The fact of the matter is we all like to receive praise and recognition because they make us feel good. I'm not being critical of that innate characteristic of our own human behavior. It is perfectly natural because we are in leadership positions on earth and have domination and rulership in our being. The key is to monitor these expressions of appreciation from others and keep them in their place. If this is not done, pride will cause you to take the gift you have and turn it into a weapon against your spiritual effectiveness and your own relationship and continued fellowship with God.

"...Yes, all of you be submissive to one another, and be clothed with humility, for 'God resists the proud, but gives grace to the humble. Therefore, humble yourselves under the mighty hand of God, that He may exalt you in due time."   *(1 Peter 5:5,6 NKJV)*

As you serve in the music ministry, I would encourage you to focus your attention on worship toward Him. He knows what each member of the body is for, and we must be content to flow in the vein for which we were created. I can tell you from personal experience that if you remain faithful to God in one area and He has gifts that He desires to use in you in other areas, He will elevate you in His perfect time without hesitation.

Unfortunately, I have witnessed individuals grow in pride and move into areas that were not meant for them, and ultimately they were not effective. As pride grows, it begins to take on a nature and personality of itself. It is no longer a child; it grows into its adolescent years and takes on another scope— it becomes rebellion.

The Ride of a Rebel

Rebellion is the action of a prideful heart. It's the next level of pride and if not checked, it will bring destruction.

"Pride goes before destruction, a haughty spirit before a fall."
(Proverbs 16:18 NIV)

The rebellious nature is one that is in complete defiance toward authority. It has made itself a god and will not relinquish its throne to anyone—not even God Himself. The final destination of a rebel, or one who defies authority, is the bottom. *"...I beheld Satan as lightning fall from heaven."* *(Luke 10:18)*

To disagree is not the same as to rebel. Disagreements can end with a peaceful, amicable conclusion or resolution of a situation, but a rebellious spirit has but one goal—to make as much noise at it can going out the door. And sadly enough, it seeks to take as many people as possible with it on its way down.

The spirit of rebellion is apparent in our adversary; although his end is certain, he remains dedicated to having as many people as he can come and join him. Keep in mind he still remembers the events that got him to this point. Most importantly, he remembers his God—given assignment. He was 'Mr. Minister of Music' and 'The Musician Extraordinaire', but now he is on his way to hell! The question you should ask yourself is would you want to be in torment alone? I think not. He at least has to feel as though he is not the only one who walked away from God willingly.

"So the great serpent was cast out, that serpent of old, called the Devil and Satan, who deceives the whole world; he was cast to the earth, and his angels were cast out with him."
(Revelation 12:9 CEV)

Keep in mind that your gift will make room for you (Proverbs 18:16); therefore, there is no need to turn your heart from the Father. Resist the temptation to follow the path that Satan started in heaven. Refuse to carry on the legacy of pride, rebellion, and ultimately destruction. You were gifted and arrayed with talents and desires for music. I admonish you to guard against your enemy. Don't turn your focus inward to your gifts, but keep them focused on He who gave you the gifts, talents, and abilities.

When the opportunity presents itself—and it surely will—to turn your focus toward something other than God, say as Jesus said, *"…Get thee hence, Satan; for it is written, Thou shalt worship the Lord thy God, and Him only shalt thou serve"* *(Matt. 4:10).* You are a part of the earthly replica of music ministry based upon the Kingdom's music model because it is a delight to the Lord. These are principles that function in complete harmony with one another, and God is delighted that you have enlisted in His earthly choir.

It is important to note that the very purpose for our creation; was to worship God. That is indeed the primary function of man. We were created *"for His pleasure" (Rev. 4:11).* Now with your gift in hand and your heart firmly focused

> *As pride grows, it begins to take on a nature and personality of itself.*

on His worship, let's continue the journey from performance to praise.

3

A Firm Foundation

As we continue to move toward excellence in our music ministry, we must move through the portal of time. As we move from eternity into the space of time as we know it, I think the most logical place to visit is the beginning of earthly music ministry.

For the record, I'm well aware that what is outlined in this chapter does not necessarily represent the very first mention of music on earth. In fact, the first mention of music in scripture was Genesis 4:21: *"And his brother's name was Jubal: he was the father of all such as handle the harp and organ..."* We could probably spend a considerable amount of time right there discussing Jubal (from which we get jubilant, jubilee, and jubilation) and his brothers Jabal and Tubal-Cain and their historical significance. We also know that when God created the universe, He put music into every part of His creation. The scripture is full of examples: the stars sing together (Job 38:7), the valleys shout for joy and sing (Psalms 65:13), the mountains break forth into singing (Isaiah 44:23), the trees sing and clap their hands (1 Chronicles 16:33), the heavens sing (Isaiah 44:23), the hills sing (Psalms 98:8), the birds sing (Psalms 104:12), the sea roars and the floods clap their hands (Psalms 98:7), and even the rocks will cry out if we don't praise the Father (Luke 19:40). All these facts are important foundational and historical truths. However, for the purposes of our discussion in this chapter, we want to examine the foundational Biblical history as it pertains to music in church as we know it today.

Now I would agree that many things have changed since the birth of music ministry, but there are some basic elements of the origin and establishment of music in the house of

God that must be reviewed. Everything has an earthly origin even though God established everything. He started it in the earth at some juncture. So that leaves us asking the questions, "Where did music in church start?" and "What principles did God establish when it began?"

The Moses Factor

There is no shortage of Sunday school stories about Moses. We are all familiar with the particulars of his journey and service to the Lord. We all know that God divinely chose him to lead His people out of Egypt. God worked awesome miracles by the hand of Moses in order to lead the Israelites out of Egypt. We are also acquainted with the saga and challenges of the children of Israel while on their way to the promised land with Moses. This leads us to examine one event in particular that would birth a nation of musicians and music ministry, as we most commonly know it today.

"And the Lord said unto Moses, 'Go get thee down; for thy people which thou broughtest out of the land of Egypt, have corrupted themselves.'"

(Exodus 32:7)

"Who is on the Lord's side?"

God was clearly upset with the children of Israel. Just think about it this way. A nation of people cried out to you to deliver them from the hands of their oppressor; not only do you bring them out, but you do it in a flamboyant way—a way that shows them and the world whose children they are and how powerful their God is for generations to come. But when the person who was designated as the spokesman, or instrument of divine deliverance, goes to commune with you, they decide to build an idol and worship it! This is a big, big, big No-no. It's likened to your preventing someone from being hit by an oncoming car and when the person recuperates, he thanks a perfect stranger for saving his life—as if this person had anything to do with him having his life spared.

How would you view such a thing? What would you

think causes this kind of behavior? I'll tell you what God says about it. "I'm a jealous God. I will have no other gods before me." (Ex. 20:3-5) The behavior resulted from selfishness and greed. God wasn't standing for it then, and He is not going to stand for it today.

As worship leaders, we must be aware of this fact throughout our ministry and lives. The "no other god before me" principle gauges the behavior of our hearts toward God. There is no way to be an active, effective part of music ministry on any level and have 'other gods' before the True and Living God. It is impossible to worship two gods simultaneously.

"No man can serve two masters: for either he will hate the one and love the other; or else he will hold to the one, and despise the other..."
(Matthew 6:24)

While Moses was up in the mountains talking to God, God told him to go down to "thy" people, indicating that He no longer claimed them as His own. When Moses and Joshua came down the mountain, Moses saw the idolatry of the Israelites, and he was extremely angry. In his anger, he broke the stones with the Ten Commandments on them and burned down the golden calf that had been made. Once he burned down the calf, Moses ground it into powder and made the first serving of Kool-Aid or Crystal Light for the diet conscious. He took the ground powder, mixed it with water, and made the Israelites drink it! Can you imagine the taste?

Afterwards, Moses asks them, *"Who is on the Lord's side? Let him come unto me"* (Exodus 32:26 KJV). What a question. After Israel had obviously turned to another god, Moses still asked if there was anyone who was still standing on the Lord's side. In other words, "Have you strayed and are you willing to come back? Have you repented in your heart?" Only one tribe out of twelve—the tribe of Levi—did not hesitate to move and stand at Moses' side.

Can you imagine the miracle of one tribe being completely on one accord as they repented and moved toward the side of Moses as an act of love toward God? Even though they had participated with the other 11 tribes and suffered the consequences, they were willing to forsake their allegiance to the other tribes and boldly say, " We are on the Lord's side." With those steps in the sand, which demonstrated their turn from idolatry to the Father, the Levites touched the heart of God in such a way that they would be placed in a position to serve and be served throughout the Tent of Meetings, or what we know today as the House of Worship or the church.

> *It is impossible to worship two gods simultaneously.*

"Of all the Israelites, I have given the Levites as gifts to Aaron and his sons to do the work at the Tent of Meeting on behalf of the Israelites and to make atonement for them so that no plague will strike the Israelites when they go near the sanctuary."

(Numbers 8:19 NIV)

God gave the Levites as gifts to Aaron. These individuals were considered gifts. Because each person is given a gift, talent, or ability at birth, God was saying that each one of these Levites had something to offer to the Tent of Meetings. For the purpose of this book, we must understand that some of those gifts made available to the Tent of Meetings were for the music department. Musicians, singers, songwriters, and others were all a part of the gifts given to Aaron for the work of the ministry.

Thus, we see the first process during which a group was selected to work in the music ministry on behalf of the rest of the tribes or people of God. The Levites were set aside and consecrated for service in the ministry. The scriptures tell us that they were ceremonially cleaned for service.

"The Lord said to Moses; 'Take the Levites from among the other Israelites and make them ceremonially clean." (Numbers 8:5,6 NIV)

It is absolutely necessary that God consecrate us for ser-

28

vice. But it is also imperative that we continue to consecrate ourselves for the service for which we have been called to provide. This self-consecration is fundamental as we continue to function and ask the Lord how He wants the service to be rendered to the people. We must make sure our consecration is coupled with an inquiry that yields to His way of doing things.

"He said to them, 'You are the heads of the Levitical families; you and your fellow Levites are to consecrate yourselves and bring up the ark of the Lord, the God of Israel, to the place I have prepared for it. It was because of you, the Levites, did not bring it up the first time that the Lord our God broke out in anger against us. We did not inquire of him about how to do it in the prescribed way."

(1 Chronicles 15: 12,13)

God's prescribed way, as it pertains to music ministry in the church, was demonstrated in 1 Chronicles 15:16: *"David told the leaders of the Levites to appoint their brothers as singers to sing joyful songs, accompanied by musical instruments: lyres, harps and cymbals."* Thus, we see the initial organized music ministry offered in scripture. Subsequent scriptures in this chapter give a more detailed account of each person's role and additional positions that we see highlighted in the music ministry today.

As we begin to move forward into additional principles of music ministry, I want us to be careful to note that the hearts of the individuals involved in music ministry are the most important aspect of service to God. As stated earlier, the Levites partook in idolatry just like their fellow tribe mates. However, God was touched by their repentant hearts and their deliberate action and swift movement towards Him as a sign of love and desire for Him.

This is the same act of commitment God is looking for today. People who are in music ministry must ask themselves the same question Moses posed to the Israelites: "Who is on the Lord's side?"

4

Priceless Principles

In case the previous question has you stumped in one way or another, I will give you the answer. The answer is, **(your name here),** *you* should be the one to confirm that you are on the Lord's side. This is a pivotal question that must be answered before you move any further in this book. You must be able to affirm to yourself and to God that you are on His side and are firmly committed to follow His order of ministry via the avenue of music.

There are numerous principles throughout scripture that are relevant to successful participation in the area of music ministry. For the sake of space and effectiveness, I have chosen to outline only five essential principles in this context. These are absolutes when we move into the realm of music ministry.

Principle #1: THOSE INVOLVED IN THE MUSIC MINISTRY ARE CHOSEN AND "SET APART."

"And David spake to the chief of the Levites to appoint their brethren to be the singers with instruments of music, psalteries and harps and cymbals, sounding, by lifting up their voice with joy."

(1 Chronicles 15:16)

"And with them Heman and Jeduthun, and the rest that were chosen, who were expressed by name, to give thanks to the LORD, because his mercy endureth forever;"

(1 Chronicles 16:41)

As we discovered in chapter three, the tribe of Levi was set apart and chosen for the task of ministry in the temple, which included the music ministry. During this period in the scriptures, musicians were chosen from the house of the tribe of Levi exclusively. Levi had three sons: Gershon, Kohath, and

Merari, from whom all who ministered in God's house would come. From these three sons came three chief musicians, who were placed over the music ministry: Asaph (Gershonite), Heman (Kohathite), and Jeduthun (Merarite); Chenaniah (Gershonite) was the overall Master of Song. This Levitical model for worship began the establishment for the blueprint or roadmap for how we look at the music ministry within the local church as we know it today.

It is safe to say that music is important to God. We can denote that as a reasonable fact because there are more than 800 scriptures that refer to music. There is no doubt that the ministry of music has God's attention. However, along with this attention come details, requirements, and a selection of people who can and will give themselves to ministry through music. Because music is high on God's list of important ministries in the church, the Father views the music ministry with a great deal of satisfaction when He witnesses the execution of these gifts according to His design and order.

> You must take an oath of separation and commitment.

In Hebrew, the word chosen is *bahar*; in the Greek, it derives from the word *eklektos.* Both words are translated to mean; *to be singled out from others for a special service.* When you, just like the Levites, make a concrete decision to take the side of allegiance for the Lord, which prompts Him to choose you to be a servant set apart to do His will among the people, understand that this appointment should not be taken lightly because you have been selected for a special service **to** the Lord. This must stay in your mind as you serve.

"And whatsoever ye do in word or deed, do all in the name of the Lord Jesus, giving thanks to God and the Father by him."

(Colossians 3:17)

Once you realize that you have been chosen and that God has set you apart or designated you for the music ministry, you will have a different view of ministering to your prospective congregation. You must realize that the first foundation of your place in ministry comes from God and is given to you to share with others.

This balance must be in place and must be recognized. The privilege God has placed on your life by giving you a particular musical gift and selecting you to be a vessel for the Father's use is a humbling one. What a wonderful place to be...chosen and set apart for the Master's use.

Principle #2: THOSE INVOLVED IN THE MUSIC MINISTRY ARE REQUIRED TO ENTER INTO AN OATH OF HOLINESS.

"And the rest of the people, the priests, the Levites, the porters, the singers, Nethinims, and all they that separated themselves from the people of the lands unto the law of God, their wives, their sons, and their daughters, every one having knowledge, and having understanding; They clave to their brethren, their nobles, and entered <u>into a curse, and into an oath</u>, to walk in God's law, which was given by Moses the servant of God, and to observe and do all the commandments of the LORD our Lord, and his judgments and his statutes;" (Nehemiah 10:28-29)

Notice in this scripture that they were actually inviting the curse of God upon themselves (and their families I might add), if they failed to keep their oath. The word *curse* is defined as a *source or cause of evil*. This denotes the seriousness of the action they were taking. If you study the Old Testament in particular, you'll find that curses were certainly nothing to play with; some of them are still around today. In taking the action of separation, they were required to enter into an oath.

"They clave to their brethren, their nobles, and entered <u>into a curse, and into an oath</u>, to walk in God's law." (Nehemiah 10:29)

The dictionary definition of the word *oath* is *a formal promise to fulfill a pledge, often calling on God as witness.* However, the word *oath* has a more substantial meaning when translated from the Hebrew language. The word *oath* in Hebrew is translated as "shebuah." This is the word from which we get the word *sheba*, which means *seven* and is the sacred number of God. It is important to note that this was a secret oath or personal commitment between them and God.

As a musician or individual involved in music ministry, you must take an oath of separation and commitment. This secret or personal commitment (oath) that you make with the Lord will be seen in your commitment and dedication to a life of holiness unto the Lord. There is a responsibility that God bestowed on each individual that entered in this oath and that responsibility still has place today. When you come to a point where you acknowledge that music is the area of ministry that you will separate yourself for and to, then you must recognize the seriousness and personal spiritual requirements that it will take for you to keep your end of the agreement, or promise for holiness, intact.

Principle #3: THOSE INVOLVED IN THE MUSIC MINISTRY ARE SKILLFUL, ANOINTED, AND TEACHABLE.

Skillfulness in any area is a gift from God. There are some who are born with specific skills. Yet others acquire skills through some formal or informal training or other avenue. No matter how a person acquires a skill, we can trace the origin of the skill back to God. With skill comes responsibility, and with responsibility comes a dedication to the area in which you are skillful.

Have you ever wondered why there are so many professional associations and organizations specific to a field of study? What is the core reason for these associations? It is their commonality to a field of study and the dedication to continue to be a part of the area that they are skillful in?

From a music ministry standpoint, we are also in an association. Each church throughout the country is a chapter. We are responsible for engaging people in our respective cities in the music ministry. God is the president of the association. He is always giving us new tunes, outlets, and ways to perfect our skills. Individuals in music have a mistaken concept that the anointing only executes skill and that God places no requirement on them to perfect the gifts, talents, and abilities that He has given to us. This is a debilitating trend of thought because the anointing has a teaching element to it as well.

*"But the anointing which ye received of him abideth in you, and ye need not that any man teach you: but as the **same anointing teacheth you of all things**, and is truth, and is no lie, and even as it hath taught you, ye shall abide in him."*   *(1 John 2:27)*

Skill and the anointing work in cooperation with each other to achieve the purposes of God. The unity among gifts is necessary to usher in the presence of God.

"Sing unto him a new song; play skillfully with a loud noise."
                                                                                    (Psalms 33:3)

Throughout the scriptures, there are several passages that highlight the relationship between skill, anointing, and teachability. (See 1 Chronicles 15:22 and 25:6-8) The ability to continue to learn and be teachable is one of the greatest assets of effective musicianship. As a participant in music ministry, you must be open to correction and never cling to a "know it all" attitude musically or spiritually. Skill is developed through practice and preparation. The anointing is not a substitute for either. We all must continue to perfect our gifts, and we will discuss this in more detail in coming chapters.

> *Skillfulness in any area is a gift from God.*

Principle # 4: THOSE INVOLVED IN THE MUSIC MINISTRY ARE FAITHFUL.

Faithfulness is very hard to ascertain from people who function in a variety of positions in our lives. It seems almost a lost cause in our current times that others will be dependable in their actions toward us. We all desire people who will stick and stay, even when things go wrong and do not happen according to the prescribed schedule. When their agenda or desires for elevation and promotion are not being realized, they remain determined and steadfast. Jumping ship is never an option, even if they secretly feel unappreciated and overlooked; they stay because faithfulness is at their core.

> *The unity among gifts is necessary to usher in the presence of God.*

In making this point real, I ask you the following questions: Have you ever felt as though God has overlooked you, your hard work, and your dedication? Have you stayed away from trouble and kept yourself separated from the other things everyone else is doing openly that are displeasing to Him? Do you come to rehearsal on time ready to give your all, but watch the solos go to the people that are always late or rarely prepared? Are you a musician who never complains and gives your all to the ministry with which you are involved, yet you are never recognized or shown appreciation for your sacrifices? The real question is if you are faithful, how do you remain faithful beyond your emotions and the natural dictates of man's nature? What is the definition of faithfulness, and what does God expect of us?

Faithfulness is a moment by moment, day by day, circumstance by circumstance decision to do one word—stay. To stay committed when you can leave is faithfulness. To remain steadfast when you are continually passed over is faithfulness. There is nothing holding you to this place you are in, and you feel looked over anyway, so just leave. It's not that simple—you've made a commitment to stay in your place until it's your turn to be moved into the next position.

"And they ministered before the dwelling place of the tabernacle of the congregation with singing, until Solomon had built the house of the Lord in Jerusalem; and they waited on their office according to their order."
(1 Chronicles 6:32)

The word "wait" in this scripture is the Hebrew word, "omad" which means to stand or stay. Imagine when people stand in a line to get their movie passes to view the latest movie at the box office. They stand there waiting on their turn to participate in the viewing of this movie. They don't move until they are in the position they desire. The end result they are expecting is to be one of the people that is shown where the theatre is that they will be able to do what they waited in line with the expectation of doing, which is to watch a movie.

> To stay committed when you can leave is faithfulness.

I am going to be honest with you when I tell you that, "Life is not fair." That statement is true. However, there is consolation in another statement. "God is just." As we serve the Lord, we are going to see and experience things that look unfair. The outcomes seem so wrong. But what is happening in and with someone else has nothing to do with you while you are standing in line waiting on your ticket to get in the theatre. Really. Just think about that. There are people who hold spaces for other people or let others cut in front of them, but my question to you is, "Does that stop you from getting your ticket and eventually getting in the movie?" The answer is — No. If you stand there, you are going to see the movie.

The same is true for God. He needs people who will just stand there until it's their turn to serve in the house of God in any given capacity. Notice the scripture also says, *"they waited on **their** office according to **their** order."*

This denotes that the place in the line and the seat once they sat down belonged to them. The place they occupied in line belonged to them. No one else could stand in his or her spot in the line. Even when someone lets someone in front of him or her, guess what? She moved her space over to let some-one else in. Did it affect your space? Yes, it did, but not from the standpoint of moving your position *toward* your final expectation.

"*...their office...*" The seat that you are going to occupy in the movie theatre belongs to someone else while they are looking at the movie, but when you enter the theatre and take a seat, that seat no longer belongs to the person that was sitting there before. God is letting you know that while you're waiting in line, He has already marked that seat or position with your name on it. Your place in the music ministry, recording industry, and life are already marked with you name on them. You may have to wait in line, and someone might have cut in front of the line, but you are still in line, and one of those seats has your name on it.

One of the other facts to consider is that God sees and rewards faithfulness. We all know the story of the prodigal son. A man has two sons; the younger son asks for his inheritance, leaves the father's house, and squanders all his money. When he has nothing, he comes back to his father's house. When he returns, his father is elated and throws a huge celebration. The older son, who stayed home, is unhappy about all the attention and extravagance being given to the son who has returned. The older son is upset because he has been faithful to the father, but has not been shown the same level of appreciation for his faithful service.

> "*They waited on **their** office according to **their** order.*"

"But he answered his father. 'Look! All these years I've been slaving for you and never disobeyed your orders. Yet you never gave me even a young goat so I could celebrate with my friends. But when this son of yours who has squandered your property with prostitutes comes home, you kill the fattened calf for him! 'My son' the father said, 'you are always with me, and everything I have is yours.'"

(Luke 15: 29-31 NIV)

The son was upset because it seemed as if the father had overlooked his faithfulness. Yes, the fattened calf was roasted, and people ate and were merry because of the son's return. This may have seemed unfair, but the bottom line is that even though a celebration was given; the son had used all of his inheritance, the blessing of faithfulness was the abiding presence of the father and knowing that everything the father had belonged to the faithful son. This my friend is just.

In my mind, there is no doubt that the father probably accumulated more wealth while the younger son was away; however, the father reaffirms that the younger son still has no part in the blessings that have been accumulated since his departure.

This parable shows us that there is great reward in standing and staying with the Father. He knows that you are standing there while others are going out doing all sorts of things outside of the precepts He has put in place. Yes, they are doing wrong and even participating in sinful acts openly, but they are still considered sons. And the justice of God says, *"You are a son and an heir to greater things that I have in the house. I know your faithfulness and I give you access to everything I have. It all belongs to you."* (Matt. 25:23)

*"So he left there before the ark of the covenant of the LORD Asaph and his brethren, to minister before the ark **continually,** as every day's work required."*   (1 Chronicles 16:37)

Faithfulness is continual. It is coming to choir rehearsal prepared because you rehearsed at home. It is playing the same chords repeatedly until you have them right. It is forsaking the quick, easy way out, refusing to give up after disagreements, or giving your all even after your way of doing things was not adopted. God needs to know that you are there for the long haul. Being faithful simply means that you will stay in your place doing the same thing continually until God moves you into another position.

Principle # 5: THOSE INVOLVED IN THE MUSIC MINISTRY STRIVE FOR UNITY.

"All the Levites who were musicians - Asaph, Heman, Jeduthun and their sons and relatives - stood on the east side of the altar, dressed in fine linen and playing cymbals, harps and lyres. They were accompanied by 120 priests sounding trumpets. The trumpeters and singers joined in unison, as with one voice, to give praise and thanks to the Lord. Accompanied by trumpets, cymbals and other instruments, they raised their voices in praise to the Lord and sang: 'He is good; his love endures forever.' Then the temple of the Lord was filled with a cloud, and the priests could not perform their service because of the cloud, for the glory of the Lord filled the temple of God."
(2 Chronicles 5:12-14 NIV)

Because of the manner in which we handle music ministry today, we cannot really appreciate the level of difficulty that was involved with all of the different elements of ministry functioning together in unity during this time in scripture. However, I believe that the glory of God was experienced because of the unity that was among the musicians.

> *Faithfulness is continual.*

The unification of instruments can never take place if there is not a unification of the heart and of purpose. The Levites were unified in their hearts before the Lord. Because of that unity, a musical miracle took place at the right side of the altar. The musicians and singers were doing something that was extremely difficult. Musically, it was a miracle that the singers and musicians played and sang "as one." Historically, the music of this time was believed to be highly improvisational (recited or composed without any prior rehearsal) and included microtonic intervals, which would have made it hard to sing "with one voice," especially with the number of musicians and singers that were involved at one time.

This scripture is a perfect example of how God blesses in the midst of unity. When everyone is unified in heart toward a common goal, which is to offer praise to God with excellence and heart felt love for Him, this unity serves as a springboard for the unification of instruments and voices, which creates an atmosphere for the glory of God to be revealed in our churches today.

"Behold how good and pleasant it is for brethren to dwell together in unity!"
(Psalms 133.1)

As these Biblical principles of music ministry foundation settle in your heart, we will examine some effective praise and worship strategies to help you with music ministry within your respective congregations. Take a breath and grab your gear...we're climbing a little higher.

5

Make It Worth Your While

Hopefully, when you decided that you had been called to the music ministry, you did so with sincerity toward the Lord and not because there were not any openings in the ministry you really wanted to become a part of. If that is the case, I would offer a suggestion that may make your stint in the music ministry an effective one: simply give it your all.

The music ministry is one of the most important ministries in the church. I reiterate that involvement in it on any level should not be taken for granted. As we move toward taking music ministry to a higher level of excellence, let's regard our attitude toward the effectiveness we render as individuals and as a collective body with a high priority.

The more effective we are in our respective positions, the more the Father will be glorified; this should be our first desire. When we take our positions seriously and make praise and worship a worthwhile experience for others, I can guarantee that God will make it a worthwhile experience for us—naturally and spiritually. The real questions that come to mind for most of us are: How can we gauge our effectiveness? Is it according to one individual's part, or is it determined by the entire group of individuals who participate? Are we taking the temperature of the congregation or of the pastor? Ultimately, what can we use to tell us whether we have pleased God and ministered to the people — effectively?

The dictionary defines the word effective as *having an intended or expected result; outcome*. So, as we examine how to determine whether we achieved the outcome we were expecting, we naturally begin with analyzing what we expected to achieve in the first place. But, before I give you some simple gauges to determine effectiveness, let me first give you the

one major DON'T. DON'T GAUGE YOUR EFFECTIVENESS
BY PEOPLE!

The primary way to gauge whether or not you are effective is to determine how you feel when everything is over.
Do you have peace within because you know that you did what
God asked of you? Don't lock yourself into how God moved
on one particular Sunday as the thermostat for how things
should happen every week. God may
manifest Himself in different ways
from Sunday to Sunday; just know
that as long as you followed His instruction for that week, that day, that
minute, and that second, you are

> *The music ministry is
> one of the most impor-
> tant ministries in the
> church.*

bound to be successful and effective in your music ministry.
Furthermore, if after praise and worship people are coming to
you, telling you what a wonderful job you did, and that's all
they seem to focus on, you might want to check your effectiveness. If, however, you hear people talking about how God
moved and manifested His presence in the service, and that,
in fact, they can't even really remember who lead worship...
they just know that God showed up! WOW! That's effective.

I also believe that you will be able to see the level of
your effectiveness within a particular congregation if you can
detect tangible growth taking place in the church. Is the church
growing, and/or is there some obvious impartation to the
people during the worship service? From a leadership standpoint, you may also detect that the music ministry of which
you are a part is effective if you can see growth within the
choir or among the praise team members. The level of your
effectiveness may need to be re-evaluated if your choir is in
the midst of chaos, confusion, and conflict.

One of the other indicators (from an abstract point of
view) is something I have experienced personally in my own
life. I often experience some of the biggest spiritual fights, at-
tacks, frustrations, and issues when I know that I have effectively done what the Father has asked me to do. When I see

the fruit of that obedience, the adversary usually sends assault my way.

Spiritual effectiveness can be detected by the revelation that is being poured out to you by the Father. Within any relationship of love and closeness, the desire to give is one of the primary indicators of the intimacy that exists between two people. Because we are created in the image of God and after His likeness (Genesis 1:26), He is without question the ultimate giver of all things. The Father freely gives spiritual gifts of impartation and anointing to us; after all, this is His work that we are administering on His behalf. I believe the closeness of your relationship with Him will be a direct reflection of the revelation, anointing, and power that is available to you and that will be manifested significantly to the fellowship in which you are involved.

Finally, a practical evaluation of where you are as it pertains to effectiveness within the music ministry is simply a matter of setting goals, revisiting those goals after a period of time, and analyzing whether or not you reached a particular goal. For example, if one of your goals is to have a multi-cultural music department, then it would stand to reason that you would see a significant presence of other cultures and nationalities within the music ministry over a period of time. Individual goals could be something as simple as making a commitment to be on time to rehearsals or taking a specific time during the week to review the material from choir rehearsal prior to singing on Sunday.

The last thing we must concretely settle in our hearts concerning music ministry effectiveness is simply the knowledge that music is a ministry, and it must be treated with that level of seriousness and commitment in order for it to be effective. Once you view your praise and worship ministry as just that— a ministry—you will inevitably sense in your heart when you are on target and when you are not.

Firm Foundation

Part of your target mindset knows that there is scriptural foundation for your position within the ministry of music (John 4:21-24). Praise and worship have distinct definitions that enable us to grasp a clear understanding of what our function is in the music ministry. Where praise is dwelling upon what God has done, worship is dwelling upon Who HE is (His deity and not just His acts). Worship says… "God if you don't do another thing for me, I honor you just because you're God and you're worthy of honor." You and I were created to worship the Father. Our life's purpose can be summed up in this simple statement at the most elementary stage of Christianity as believers. *"This people have I formed for myself; they shall shew forth my praise" (Isaiah 43:21).* In this scripture, we see no evidence of a pro-choice option. God Himself declares that the reason we were formed in the first place was to actively demonstrate the praises of God. As believers who say we extol the name of God, this is not an optional act. *"I beseech you therefore, brethren, by the mercies of God, that you present your bodies a living sacrifice, holy, acceptable unto God, which is your reasonable service" (Romans 12:1).*

There is no way I want to give you an unrealistic impression that you will always feel like praising and worshipping God. You are human, just as the congregation is human, and there will be days when neither you nor those you are leading into the presence of God will want to go. But there is grace available to you as a person in music ministry to make the shift from being one who wants to follow to one called to lead. These are the times when you will see your greatest level of effectiveness because God always answers a sacrifice with a greater manifestation of His power.

> *"This people have I formed for myself; they shall shew forth my praise."*
> *(Isaiah 43:21)*

As a person called as a leader on the frontlines of praise and worship, take hold of the variety of expressions God accepts as an act of praise and worship toward Him. It is your responsibility to convey to the fellowship a variety of ways to praise and worship the Father. This can be one aspect of your goal setting. When you see the fellowship utilizing these expressions, this will give your congregation the necessary freedom to express their heartfelt worship and indicate that you are indeed making a difference in the flow of worship for that congregation. You are providing liberty of expression when you teach the congregation other ways to express their worship and praise to God. This is the ultimate indicator of an effective music ministry.

Here are some expressions of praise and worship responses:

EXPRESSIONS OF PRAISE (Hebrew)

BARAK -	To kneel, bless, or salute
YADAH -	Lifted hands; Thankful expression
TOWDAH -	Sacrifice of praise (What God is going to do)
ZAMAR -	Instrumental praise
SHABACH -	Shout or address in a loud tone; triumph
HALAL -	To boast, be clamorously foolish; celebrate
TEHILLAH -	High praise, to sing and laud

WORSHIP RESPONSES

HANDS -	Clapping, Lifting, Giving
VOICE -	Singing, Shouting, Praising, Boasting, Praying
BODY -	Bowing, Kneeling, Dancing, Stillness
MUSIC -	Instruments, New Songs, Call & Response
WILL -	Confession, Self-examination, Awe

Leading praise and worship can be one of the most difficult ministries in the church. Imagine trying to usher an entire congregation, comprised of those who are tired, sick, hurting, stubborn, lazy, unteachable, or in some other state, into the very presence of the Almighty God on an individual and congregational level. Needless to say, it can be an extremely daunting task! This is why you must know that you are called and anointed for this ministry. Though we will discuss this later, I must note right here that your most gifted singer may not be the most qualified worship leader. It is a unique anointing. Be careful about putting the most talented person you have out front and making the assumption that that person is necessarily the one for the job.

Always keep in mind that praise and worship should be an active, participatory, and integral part of the worship service. The congregation should not be spectators; they should become active participants. This is why God has given us so many ways to express our praise to Him. He loves to see the activity of our limbs in total expression and response to His wonderful faithfulness and indescribable awesomeness. When your goal is to bring this level of worship to the congregation Sunday after Sunday, and your heart is set toward seeing that the Father is glorified by seeking obedience to Him, then be confident in the fact that you are a part of a nucleus that is moving in the body of Christ with effectiveness and power.

6

From One Leader to Another

Praise and worship is a ministry that has a unique and specific calling and requires special gifts and skills that are different than those of musicians, choir members, lead vocalists, pastors, etc. The worship leader is an individual called and anointed by God to minister in the house of God by leading the people of God into His presence.

Jesus planted a spiritual mandate in the earth when he declared, *"Believe me, woman, a time is coming when you will worship the Father neither on this mountain nor in Jerusalem. You Samaritans worship what you do not know; we worship what we do know, for salvation is from the Jews. Yet a time is coming and has now come when true worshipers will worship the Father in spirit and truth, for they are the kind of worshipers the Father seeks. God is spirit, and his worshipers must worship in spirit and in truth."(John 4:21-24)* This is the foundation for the act of worship among the House of God to the Father. Today is the day that we must worship in spirit and in truth.

Our English word for *worship* (worthship) is defined as *to ascribe worth or value to.* Worthiness of the one receiving special honor or devotion, reverent devotion, and allegiance are not predicated on who is giving the worship. It is authenticated in this case by Who is being worshipped. The most commonly used Greek word for worship is ***proskuneo***, which actually means *to prostrate oneself before God; to show extreme fondness and unwavering devotion; and to submit oneself in adoration.* It means *to kneel or fall down in homage.* The act of worship is, in fact, responding to all God is with all that we are! In this context, it is based on the relationship that we have with the Lord. The truth of worship is that it is always being done toward something. We were created to worship. It is the cornerstone of what we were innately created to do. There-fore, the question is what or who are you worshipping? Even if your worship is not turned toward the Father, rest assured, you are worshipping something. Every worship leader should be cognitively aware of this fact because it will help you as you lead others to direct their worship toward the Father.

As should be expected with any position of leadership, there is a greater amount of responsibility. The tasks some-times are more tedious, and they also take forethought and consideration. All the same principles are true as they relate to the responsibilities of a worship leader. In addition, leaders are placed under a different type of scrutiny when something goes wrong, and believe me, you will know when something goes wrong! As a leader, you will feel it, and others will let you know.

A great deal of the time you will feel underappreciated for all the time, effort, and energy you devote to preparing for what seems to be just a three hour function that is vital to the flow of the overall service(s) on Sunday. This is common and can only be accepted by knowing that all the time you spend behind the scenes can only truly be appreciated by the Father, who sees all of your labors of love.

"Remembering without ceasing your work of faith, and labour of love, and patience of hope in our Lord Jesus Christ, in the sight of God and our Father." *(1 Thessalonians 1:3)*

In this chapter, we will sit down and discuss function and atti-tude as they pertain to a worship leader. My role in this chapter is to serve as a motivator of excellence and encourager of grace. By the end of this chapter, I hope to have accomplished one goal... to have expressed to you the heart of God where your position in His kingdom musically is concerned. Then, I hope you will evaluate your individual effectiveness by identifying areas that need attention and those with which you are satisfied.

Who are you worshipping?

Functionality

Knowing your function in any position in life is crucial. If you don't know what your role is, then how will you know what or how you are expected to perform? With that in mind, I have highlighted what I believe are the three basic functions of a worship leader.

The first function is *to lead the entire congregation into the presence of God.* The congregation is looking to you to do what you are in position to do.... lead. They come in expecting to have a supernatural encounter with the Father during every service. You must be constantly aware that these people that are sitting and standing before you represent a variety of backgrounds, households, and situations for which they need God to get through and overcome. For many, this time of praise and worship is a lifesaver for them, and it is up to you to facilitate the encounter they need with the Father through what you do musically in each service.

The second function is *to coordinate and cover the praise team and musicians.* Coordinating and covering are two separate functions that work together. Coordinating is helping the praise team, musicians, and choir (if applicable) to harmoniously function as one unit. Covering them is to take a role that is over or in front of them. These two activities are essential because you are responsible for what is taking place on the platform musically at all times. Make sure you understand the basic principles of music and the ministry of singers and musicians because these principles will assist you in getting things in order to create a flow during the service. There should be minimal confusion if you have coordinated things efficiently, and this will give you the confidence to step out in front to lead the people of God in worship.

Let's look at the function of leading worship from a Biblical point of view by considering Miriam's actions after the Israelites watched the Egyptian army being drowned in the Red Sea. The scripture says, "...*Miriam took the tambourine in her hand and, all the women followed her with tambourines and dancing. And Miriam led them in singing…"* (Exodus 15:20 emphasis mine)

The point is that we can see the principle of leading in action; Miriam was obviously familiar with the musical basics, and she was confident as she led other women into praise and worship before God. And notice that the women followed her in singing to the Lord.

The third function is *to prepare the congregation for the delivery of the Word.* It is vitally important that you are one in spirit and mind with the leadership of the church. It is your responsibility to make sure you are aware of and familiar with the pastor's vision and that you understand the direction in which God is leading the church. When the power of agreement is operating among any group of people, the result will be the manifestation of God's presence during the service. The congregation can sense if there is strife between the worship leader and the leadership. It is imperative that you focus on the need of the people to have an intimate encounter with God during the worship service because it is the time when the soil of the heart is softened and/or broken up so that the word of God can take root in their spirits.

There is a unique and vital connection between the worship leader and the pastor. The last thing you want is a popularity contest to emerge because the music ministry or congregation has divided loyalties. The best way to make sure people are clear of the mantel of authority of the house in which you serve is to have clear actions toward the pastor's authority and make sure you require others to do the same. If people see you operating under this authority, they will naturally follow suit. Make sure you are in a position spiritually that you want the hand of God to be on the pastor.

"And Elisha said, 'As the Lord of hosts, liveth, before who I stand, surely, were it not that I regard the presence of Jehoshaphat the king of Judah, I would not look toward thee, nor see thee. But now bring me a minister. And it came to pass, when the minstrel played, that the hand of the Lord came upon him." (2 Kings 3:14-15)

If there is contention between yourself and the leadership of the church, the first thing to do is to try to work out the differences by submitting yourself to the leadership and by expressing your concerns in an open and honest fashion. If you have a more severe case, you might need to go to the Father to determine whether this is the church in which you would be best suited to serve in the kingdom of God.

Know this. Agreement is such a powerful spiritual principle that it is really essential to operating in the supernatural realm of God. When the pastor, the worship leader, and the other music ministry staff are on one accord, then you can confidently expect God to move in wondrous ways to meet the needs of His people because you are operating within the principle of agreement. But, this manifestation begins largely with your attitude as a worship leader.

*"All the Levites who were musicians - Asaph, Heman, Jeduthun and their sons and relatives - stood on the east side of the altar, dressed in fine linen amd playing cymbals, harps and lyres. They were accompanied by 120 priests sounding trumpets. The trumpeters and singers joined in **unison, as with one voice,** to give thanks to the Lord. Accompanied by the trumpets, cymbals and other instruments, they raised their voices in praise to the Lord and sang: 'He is good; his love endures forever." Then the temple of the Lord was filled a cloud, and the priests could not perform their service because of he cloud, **for the glory of the Lord filled the temple of God."***
(2 Chronicles 5:12-14 NIV)

*"Again I say unto you, **that if two of you shall agree** on earth as touching any thing that they shall ask, it shall be done for them of my Father which is in heaven. For where two or three are gathered together in my name, there am I in the midst of them."*   *(Matthew 18:19-20)*

*"And when the day of Pentecost was fully come, they **were all with one accord in one place.** And suddenly there came a sound from heaven as of a rushing mighty wind, and it filled all the house where they were sitting."*
(Acts 2:1-2)

Attitude Determines Altitude

Your disposition is crucial to the way people perceive you. It will convey your inner feelings and content of your heart. The attitude of a person, whether good or bad, is infectious, so be positive and enthusiastic. Have you ever noticed that when someone smiles at you, you tend to smile back? Just think of how the glory and joy of the Lord is being spread to the congregation as you smile during your time of worship and praise. If you don't smile, the congregation won't either, so you need to set an example for them to follow. Besides, it's better to lead people who appear to enjoy worshipping and praising God.

Your disposition or attitude should also signify control. Give strong direction and don't appear timid. Let me caution you here; giving strong direction is not the same as being mean. Trust me, I've seen some mean worship leaders who would be much better suited for body guard ministry rather than leading worship. Don't take your emotions out on the congregation. Nobody likes to be treated inappropriately, but you must take charge. Remember you are a leader, and insecurity destroys creativity. You leave yourself no room to be creative in worship if you are afraid of the people you are leading. The same is true with those who are under you in the music department. You will lose your creative edge and ultimately respect from your peers if you don't function with an attitude of confidence and authority. The bottom line is if you were called to lead, then do it with confidence.

As you stand to lead the congregation in worship, it is important that you set the example for active involvement, such as hand clapping, shouting, and lifting of the hands. You should always lead with your voice and not be afraid of the first note that comes from your mouth. If at all possible, stick with the melody of a song, it will make

Your disposition is crucial to the way people perceive you.

your job easier.

Make a mental note to make sure you are giving clear directions to the praise team members and the congregation. For instance, with praise team members, keep your hand signals simple and easy to follow. However, for the congregation, staying slightly ahead of the verse is important because they will not know where you are going if they don't know what you're looking for. If they are clear about what you want from them next, they tend to respond very well. Another tip pertains to new songs with which the congregation is not familiar with. It is helpful to say the words of the song before singing it so that they can familiarize themselves with the words as they learn to put the melody with them. Again, this method will require you to lead vocally.

Last, make sure you are leading the congregation to the Lord. I say that because you must make sure that you are not leading worship in a way that causes the congregation to draw its heart toward you. You should make every effort to lead in a way that draws the mind and heart of the people to the Lord. As you do this, you will want to make sure you open your eyes and make eye contact with the congregation. Let them see the sincerity of your heart as you encourage and exhort them to join you as you worship the Father. This tends to sway people from placing too much emphasis on you and turns their attention toward the Lord, who you are worshipping with them.

7

Give Me An "S"

When I think of the preparation of a worship leader, I generally think of four words that begin with the letter "S": Sanctification, Submission, Sensitivity, and Skill. In this chapter, we will look at each of these words and how they pertain to the preparation of worship leaders

Sanctification

The Greek word for sanctification is *hagiasmos*, which means *separation or setting apart*. In Hebrew the word is *qodesh*, which has a similar meaning that denotes "a separation from the secular and sinful and setting apart for a sacred purpose." The meaning is relatively the same in the English language as well.

Now we must examine what it means to be set apart for a sacred use. In chapter three, we came to understand the origin of the Levitical priesthood and position within the temple. It was very clear that one of the first things God did was to sanctify them for service in the Tent of Meetings, or the House of God as we would refer to it today. That prescribed order of sanctification, or the setting apart, is still important for us to realize today. Anyone involved with ministry must be aware of the prerequisite of sanctification. There is a level of sanctification that God will perform, but there is also an ongoing process of sanctification we must complete as we lead people into the presence of God.

Do you really believe that God wants you to lead His people into His presence if you are entangled with things that He has no part of? Is it really fair to say that God is accepting worship from you when you aren't separate from the secular and sinful? This is not an observation of judgment; it is simply intended to clarify the privileges and prerequisites established by God to make sure that you and I accept the position of worship leader with a complete and correct understanding of the sacredness of such a call and regard it with proper understanding and appreciation.

"Now may the very God of peace Himself sanctify you completely; and may your whole spirit, soul, and body be preserved blameless at the coming of our Lord Jesus Christ."   (I Thessalonians 5:23 NKJV)

Worship leaders have a responsibility to keep themselves in a position that is set apart for the purpose of leading people into the presence of a Holy God. We should not take this issue lightly. If we made this area a fundamental priority, I believe we would see God move more powerfully and more often in our churches today.

Remember Paul stated in 1 Corinthians 9:27, *"But I keep under my body, and bring it into subjection: lest that by any means, when I have preached to others, I myself should be a castaway."* Most people would limit their thinking and context of this scripture to sexual sins, but the term <u>my body</u> is not limited to a sexual activity of sin. We can infer this because Paul was a eunuch, which meant sex was not his issue at all. Maybe lying was his issue. Maybe it was strife or anger. Maybe he was a thief. Who knows? However, he was very frank in expressing the fact that although he was the leader, the preacher, and the one who was jailed for the cause of Christ, that he had to keep his body, mind, will, and emotions in check because he had some issues to deal with.

"And lest I should be exalted above measure through the abundance of revelations, there was given to me a thorn in the flesh...."
                                                        (2 Corinthians 12:7)

Paul was a perfect example that there is something in each of us that can present a challenge whether we want to admit it or not. The key is staying on top of it and making sure that it does not allow us to be moved from our sacred call.

The biggest deceit where music ministry and worship leaders are concerned is the deception that says just because you continue to function in a position means that God is accepting your worship. Saul was an excellent example of a person rejected by God, yet who was still going through the motions of worship.

"Now I beg you, forgive my sin and come back with me, so that I may worship the Lord.' But Samuel said to him, 'I will not go back with you. You have rejected the word of the Lord, and the Lord has rejected you as king over Israel!' Saul replied, 'I have sinned. But please honor me before the elders of my people and before Israel; come back with me, so that I may worship the Lord your God.' So Samuel went back with Saul, and Saul worshiped the Lord." (1 Samuel 15: 25 & 26, 30 & 31 NIV)

This is not a place in which worship leaders should find themselves. This is why at the core of our lives, we must have a sincere relationship with the Father. A personal relationship would prevent this kind of fiasco from ever being birthed in our lives. Always honor the sanctification that God has deliberately placed on your life. It is precious and must be guarded. The understanding of sanctification will move you into the grace of submission.

Submission

Submission is *the act of submitting or surrendering to the power of another; the quality or state of carrying out the wishes of others (obedience and surrender).* This is a rather simple explanation of what God is looking for out of you as a worship leader—obedience and surrender. We have previously discussed the leadership aspects of working with and submitting to the authority of the visionary of the house of worship. But some things can never be conveyed enough.

Make sure your heart is submitting to the leadership and pastor of the church. Make it a priority to be clear on the vision and direction of the congregation. Once you are clear, make sure you flow with that vision, even if you have another agenda in mind. The blessing will come with your surrender to the wishes and desires of the leadership God has placed over you. If the pastor asks for a specific song to be sung, then sing that song.

I know you're thinking, "I already had my songs picked." That's great. Use them next week. But you are obligated to be obedient to the request that was given to you. That, my friends, is the art of submission, which includes surrendering your agenda to follow the agenda of another and displaying the obedience to carry out what is asked of you regardless of your opinion.

The same two thoughts apply when it pertains to the Holy Spirit. Your level of submission is crucial because it is a mirror of your sensitivity to the Holy Spirit. If the Holy Spirit tells you to do something, will you surrender and obey? Or, will you behave in the same way in which you responded when the pastor wanted you to change the songs you had planned?

Sensitivity

Sensitivity is defined from a negative and positive sense. It can mean to be easily offended or touchy (negative), or it means a capability to perceive (positive). In this case, we are referring to the capability to perceive.

"But when he the Spirit of truth, comes, he will guide you into all truth. He will not speak on his own; he will speak only what he hears, and he will tell you what is yet to come."   *(John 16:13 NIV)*

Understanding the function of the Holy Spirit is vital to your receiving instruction and direction from Him. He was sent to tell you what the Father knows and desires of you. He is able to tell you what pleases the Father, and for a worship leader, this is the ultimate goal.

> *Submission is the act of submitting or surrendering to the power of another.*

A sensitivity to the move of the Holy Spirit will only be developed as you spend time with the Lord and obey the leading of the Holy Spirit in other areas of your life. Even the smallest instruction obeyed as conveyed by the Holy Spirit is an exercise in sensitivity, which will benefit you many, many times over once your spirit is fully equipped to hear and obey what it hears in the spirit realm.

I must admit, that maturity in this area takes some time, but if your heart is in a place where you sincerely want to hear from the Father, especially as it pertains to the level of ministry He wants you to provide, I assure you, He will make His wishes known to you. His desire is to feed you with His heart directly from the throne of God so that His people will manifest and return to Him His level of worship.

Always wait on direction from the Holy Spirit. It will save you time and will cause you to be effective in your ministry as a worship leader. A quick way to summon the Holy Spirit is....you guessed it—worship! So, if you worship in your private time, it will cause you to be sensitive to His leading in your public time.

Skill

Skill is proficiency (progressive in an area of learning, vocation or art) or dexterity.

In this section, we will briefly discuss the components of building your skill level and the importance of giving attention to the amount of time you spend practicing, rehearsing, and developing your gifts and abilities.

You must understand two things. First, gifting does not supercede practice and work. *"Study to show yourselves approved unto to God..." (2 Timothy 2:15).* This applies to the music ministry gifts and oratorical gifts, such as teaching and preaching. We are responsible for refining our gifts. As a matter of fact, when God sees you taking the extra effort to perfect the gifts that He has given to you, I believe you are a candidate to receive additional gifts and additional manifestations of creativity and skill.

"...you have been faithful over a few things, I will make you ruler over many things...."   *(Matthew 25:23 NKJV)*

Second, you must PRACTICE, PRACTICE, PRACTICE. You cannot just continue to skip through the tulips and not spend the necessary time it takes to make the music and songs you render to the Lord perfect. In order to convey to others the importance of practice you must have a stong work ethic. For the purpose of this book, this is a subject that needs to be incorporated into another area of discussion, but I encourage you to ask yourself one question: Do you want the surgeon who has performed the same procedure 10 times or 100 times to operate on you? Why? It goes without saying that practice makes perfect! Then the question is does God deserve a perfect praise?

According to 1 Chronicles 15: 22, *"And Chenaniah, chief of the Levites, was for song: he instructed about the song, because he was skilfull."* Chenaniah held this responsibility not because he was related to the pastor or because he had a "good heart"; it was because he was skillful. In the church we are often intimidated by this word; however, we should not be. Often times, the choir becomes the "catch-all" ministry in the church.

> Always wait on direction from the Holy Spirit.

When we're really not sure where people should serve, well, there's always the choir! I've taught in many places, and just mentioning the word "audition" makes everyone so quiet that you could hear a pin drop! Audition? In the church? I hope so. Let's look at the logic for a moment. Hmmm, let's see. This is a choir, and in the choir we...sing. So, why is it wrong for me to inquire as to whether or not you can... sing? To some, this may seem comical, but all too often we fall in love with people's hearts without taking the time to also evaluate skill. Do you have a basic, fundamental competence level in the area you wish to participate in? Don't be scared of skill. Likewise, don't build your music ministry exclusively around someone's skill, but make sure to give it the priority and importance it deserves.

Think about it. We demand skill in every other field of service. Whether it is your mechanic, your hair stylist, your doctor, your attorney, or your dry cleaner, you want to know that the people who provide service to you know what they are doing! You insist on it. How much more should it be so in the House of God?

Growing up, I remember times when soloists would get up to sing in church, and they would say, "Pray for me as I attempt to sing this song." Huh? As you *attempt* to sing? What was really being said was, "Please overlook these mistakes I'm about to make because I'm really not prepared like I should be." Think about it. You wouldn't accept that anywhere else. Imagine if you were on a plane getting ready to take off and your pilot spoke over the intercom system and said, "Pray for me as I attempt to fly this plane." I don't know about you, but I'd get off that plane! Make sure you take the time to prepare.

8

"Perfection In Action"
Practically Speaking

For this book, we will not delve into a theological debate concerning the attributes of perfection. However, we will define the desire to give God our best in every area of our lives as an act that is befitting His majesty. Therefore, we will begin to look at many of the practical components of musicianship as they pertain to the ministry.

We will systematically begin to move through the various aspects of the roles, challenges, and solutions that individuals face while involved in music ministry. Several of the items that we discuss in the coming chapters will also be provided in the reference section of this book and in greater detail in the companion workbook/journal, which is a partner to this book. But right now, let us pick up where we left off in reference to the worship leader's role in a service.

In the previous chapters, we really looked at some of the characteristics that should or should not be present in reference to the worship leader's attitude, function, and preparation. At this point, we are going to look at some practical strategies worship leaders can implement to make their jobs easier and increase their overall level of effectiveness.

1)   *Know your musicians, singers, and/or soundtracks.*
By now, you know I am a stickler about the necessity of practicing your material. Look, if you and your musicians have not practiced, then you will not know key elements that help your ministry function at its best on Sunday. Once you have chosen your songs, practicing with your musicians, singers, and/or soundtracks allows you to flush out problems or unexpected surprises before you minister. For example, select-

ing the appropriate key for the songs you will be ministering is something that can be nailed down when you get together with the musical component of the ministry. It also affords you the opportunity to perfect the simplicity of your hand signals for items such as tempo changes, modulations, new keys, special directions with a song, or volume changes at certain times within the song.

Another item that can be perfected within this time is the all-important transition between songs. The more you know your singers and musicians, the better you will be able to change from one song to another with a seamless ease that is noticed or better yet <u>not</u> noticed by the congregation.

2)   *Don't spend too much time talking.*

Communication is key within the context of leading a congregation into worship. Therefore, it is your job to encourage them during the time of worship. You must not assume everybody understands what is going on when you are up before the fellowship. You must consider the fact that you may have new people who are unfamiliar with your style of worship or are 'unchurched' and have never experienced the dynamics of a worship service before in the congregation.

And, even though it is necessary for you to talk to the people as you minister, you must realize that you can break the flow of worship with too much dialogue, especially at the wrong point within the time set aside for worship. Be careful that when you do speak that your words are edifying to the Body and that they are not of an offensive nature. You are not the spiritual authority; you must leave the rebukes and chastisement to the pastor because that is a part of their spiritual office.

3)   *Choose your songs carefully.*

As a worship leader, you must seek to create an experience of worship for the congregation. It is not to be viewed as a one shot deal from song to song; do not skip from one song to another without any sense of purpose for the worship portion of the service. I encourage you to attempt to develop and accomplish something in worship.

When you look at the overall picture of what you are trying to achieve within the service, be sure to consider your song selection in a way that causes you to maintain a flow between songs. For instance, when a puzzle is being pieced together, the pieces that fit and click are the ones that create the picture you see on the box. The same is true for the songs and picture of the experience you are trying to achieve through your music ministry. Be careful with things like theme, tempo, and key changes because some songs simply don't go together.

The best thing you can do to alleviate this problem is to learn medleys or sets of songs that go together both spiritually and musically. Again, this will help you maintain a flow between songs. Whatever you do, try to get away from stopping after every song!

Also spend time with the pastor to make sure you understand what God is saying to the church. Is there a theme? What is the pastor's message? You can then prayerfully align the music with that message or theme.

For Their Benefit

For the benefit of the congregation, you must be conscious of the key in which you sing. This is important because if you sing in a key that is within your vocal

> *The Holy Spirit is our guide, teacher, and comforter.*

range, but is too high for the people to sing along with you, they may not participate, and that is not the goal of the worship leader. With that in mind, worship songs are generally sung in lower keys than praise songs. As a courtesy, sing in lower ranges whenever possible to increase your congregation's participation levels.

One final note, be careful not to select songs that have a high word content in them or songs that have extended solo verses to them. These are other ways in which you can fail to engage the congregation in praise and worship, and as stated earlier, that defeats the purpose of the worship leader's core goals and objectives for the worship experience.

4)   *Know your music.*

Let me say that we will deal more directly with the aspects of this section in a separate chapter. However, I will make a few clear statements that will be explained further later on.

Knowing your music is so important and I would dare say it is just plain fair! Do NOT practice on the congregation. Know the songs you are going to minister with inside out. Don't wait to stand before the congregation to begin rehearsing a song that you have not learned or are not familiar with. This creates a haven for confusion, and let me remind you that your adversary loves that! He is comfortable in confusion, and once confusion is present, it will be quite difficult for the congregation to focus wholly on God. The bottom line is be prepared!

5)   *Provide strong leadership*

I exhausted the subject of leadership in a previous chapter, but some things bear repeating again. For instance, you cannot push the leadership responsibilities on anyone else. You are the leader, so don't try to make the choir, congregation, or musicians do what you are supposed to do. You were called to lead worship, so lead worship.

Once you have clear direction from the Holy Spirit, move with confidence in the ability that God has graced your life with for this position. Flow in the fact that as you lead others, God will lead you. You can't go wrong if you stay in tune with the Holy Spirit as a worship leader.

6)   *Be sensitive to the flow and timing of the Holy Spirit.*

The Holy Spirit is our guide, teacher, and comforter. Not one of His roles in our lives is to do harm to us. Therefore, following Him is the greatest requirement as a worship leader. With that said, don't be afraid to sing a chorus or verse several times or embrace the silence of the moment. Never be in a hurry to go to the next song. There are different waves of worship. Just as you must know how to start and flow with a song, you must also be sensitive to understanding when a song needs to end. Continuing a song when the flow of worship is moving into another direction or because you like it detracts from the effectiveness of that particular song. If you like the song, sing it in the car, but know when enough is enough in the worship service.

I know it may sound impossible, but you can be prepared and sensitive to the Holy Spirit at the same time. It is like chewing gum and riding a bike. One does not hinder the function of the other; these two functions of a worship leader are not mutually exclusive to each other. Preparation requires

> *You must seek to create an experience of worship for the congregation.*

that you focus your attention on the Holy Spirit in a set way as you prepare to come before the people. However, His assistance to you changes when you are on the platform in front of people. That is why you and I cannot afford to put God in a box. He may do something completely different from your original plans. If He asks you to sing one song for the entire service, you must be open to doing that. Also, keep in mind that it is permissible to change the mood of a service as needed and directed by the Holy Spirit. For instance, you may have the women sing one chorus or the men sing a chorus acappella. Change is good, but don't get so "lost in the Spirit" that you don't have a clue about what is going on around you. You have to be "found in the flow" of what is happening around you because you will need to keep an eye on the pastor for specific instructions. He or she will know when something is appropriate and inappropriate.

The bottom line is to tune in to the leading of Holy Spirit because He is the One who can convey to you the heart of worship from the Father. The goal is to be available to Him, and He will make sure He leads you. With a wonderful worship experience comes a complete dependency on the Spirit of God.

"My sons do not be negligent now, for the Lord has chosen you to stand before Him, to serve Him, and that you should minister to Him, and burn incense." (2 Chronicles 29:11 NKJV)

9

"Perfection In Action"
Know Your Road

Up to this point, we have dealt a great deal with the spiritual aspect of the music ministry—and as well it should be because this is about ministry on a spiritual level before it is about anything else. But there is another side to music ministry that directly affects the overall effectiveness of the music ministry on a very natural or secular level. We will cover those areas in the following chapters.

You will also find that this chapter will offer a series of questions that you must answer with respect to your individual ministry situation. Not every music ministry is comprised of the same components, so please take note that if your particular situation does not warrant a particular area of discussion, then it may behoove you to read it for informational purposes, but be sure to re-read the sections that apply more directly to your particular ministry objectives.

WHERE PURPOSE IS NOT KNOWN, ABUSE IS INEVITABLE

It might surprise you to know that many people serve in roles of leadership in a church and have no idea what the vision/mission of the church in which they serve is. It is amazing how many people don't have a clue what the overall spiritual objectives for the congregation are. An unsuccessful alliance between church leadership is often the result when there is no clear vision for the direction a ministry is taking.

For the sake of argument, let's say you have a clear vision for what the pastor of your local assembly is trying to accomplish. Then I pose the next question: What is the vision for the music ministry? Even if you are not in a leadership role within the music ministry, you should be able to articulate the heart of the musical leadership as it reflects the over-all goals of the church.

Within my own music ministry and when I am mentoring or developing someone else's music ministry, there are three things I do immediately in order to bring some continuity to the spiritual road I am about to travel. Fundamentally, it is imperative for you to identify the scripture on which you will anchor the music department, clearly articulate your purpose for the music ministry, and think through your vision or mission statement. Make sure you write each of these things down, distribute them to all who are involved with the music ministry, and give a copy to the pastor so that he is aware of the direction the music department is taking in concert with his objectives for the ministry.

"And the LORD answered me, and said, Write the vision, and make it plain upon tables, that he may run that readeth it." (Habakkuk 2:2)

On the following page is a sample copy of one of the documents I developed for a particular ministry. It helped me tremendously then and continues to give me invaluable direction as I assist ministries today. I cannot stress to you how important it is for you to have a planned course spiritually. Having this written compass will even help you during difficult times, because it will function as a tangible reminder of your purpose within the particular ministry situation you are in. And if you happen to get sidetracked this is a perfect tool to bring your thoughts and goals back in line with the spiritual agenda that God has placed in your heart as it pertains to the music ministry of which you are apart.

Finally, make sure you spend some quiet, quality time with the Lord because what you are seeking for is His direction in this area of ministry. He is the only one who can accurately and concretely speak to your heart about this matter. He has a plan for the music ministry where you are and believe me, He is eager to reveal it to you. Be patient and discover the purposes He has planned for you as you become a catalyst for an excellent duplicate of the heavenly host of worhippers that surround His throne.

As you examine the layout and purpose of my vision for the above ministry, take time to consult the Father regarding where he wants your music ministry to go and how He wants you to get there. The great thing about God is that He is willing to give you the direction you need as you seek Him in this area.

The scriptural foundation is simple; it is the focal scripture for everything you do. God must give it to you because He knows where you are going. This will be an easy task if your heart and spirit are open to hear His voice.

Purpose is defined as *a deliberate intention; aim or goal; reason.* What is your intention for the music ministry? Ask yourself why will you do what you do? What are your intentions or goals for the outcome of a successful ministry? Answering these questions will assist you in conveying your purpose for the music ministry.

Last, your mission or vision should be a direct reflection of your honor and reverence for the Lord. It should also reflect the vision of the church leadership. From a musical perspective, your mission should also consider the sound and style of the services. Furthermore, it should make sure it allows for diversity and creative expression while keeping in step with the pulse of the people for whom it is designed to minister.

I cannot stress enough the importance of getting a clear picture of where you are going with the music ministry. I encourage you to quiet yourself and hear His direction. I can assure you in the long-term you will be glad you did!

On the following page write your scriptural foundation, purpose and vision/mission in the space provided.

**IF YOU DON'T CARE WHERE YOU'RE GOING,
THEN ANY ROAD WILL GET YOU THERE!**

Scriptural Foundation:

It came even to pass, as the trumpeters and singers were as one, to make one sound to be heard in praising and thanking the LORD; and when they lifted up their voice with the trumpets and cymbals and instruments of music, and praised the LORD, saying, For he is good; for his mercy endureth for ever: that then the house was filled with a cloud, even the house of the LORD; So that the priests could not stand to minister by reason of the cloud: for the glory of the LORD had filled the house of God. (2 Chronicles 5:13-14)

Purpose:

The music ministry is to act as a vehicle to usher in the presence of God. It is to set and establish an atmosphere that is conducive to worship, enabling (a) the presence of God to move freely among the congregation and (b) each person in the congregation to experience Christ on a personal level. The music ministry should serve as an enhancement to the worship service (NOT a distraction), preparing the people for the delivery of the Word of God. It is not an end in itself, but neither is it a means of filling gaps in the worship experience. The music ministry should not be used as a piece of scenic background, but rather as an active, participatory, and integral part of the worship service.

Vision/Mission:

As a music ministry, our primary mission is to magnify and glorify Jesus Christ (Colossians 3:16 - 17) in everything we do. Furthermore, it is also the mission of the music ministry to facilitate the fulfillment of the overall mission and vision of this church through the delivery of: (A) Spiritual and spirit-led music that enhances the worship service; (B) Anointed music that edifies, inspires, and challenges the body of Christ and further enables them to experience Christ on a personal level; (C) Thought-provoking and intelligent music that continues to raise the level of consciousness of the people to the awesome nature of the God we serve through praise and worship; (D) Christ-centered music that boldly shares the "Good News" with those who are lost; (E) Dynamic, multifaceted music for a diverse congregation that will not be mired in mediocrity or tradition, but continues to push the edges of the envelope so that effective ministry can take place in any atmosphere and at anytime; (F) Innovative, fresh, and creative music that is unique to this church; and (G) Training that equips, empowers, and enables others to grow and realize their full potential in the area of music ministry.

Scriptural Foundation:

_____
_____
_____
_____
_____
_____
_____
_____
_____
_____

Purpose:

_____
_____
_____
_____
_____
_____
_____
_____
_____
_____
_____
_____

Vision/Mission:

_____
_____
_____
_____
_____
_____
_____
_____
_____
_____
_____

10

Coordinate the Components

We discussed the importance of the leader's role in creating a fluid atmosphere in worship in one of the previous chapters. Someone must also be in charge of the administrative components of the music ministry. If you are that designated individual, then you must not shy away from the responsibility that has been assigned to you. On the other hand, if you are someone involved in music ministry, it is mandated by God that you give your all in service to Him. Keeping your focus on worshipping and serving the Father will enable you to submit to the leadership paradigms that are in place. The goal is to set structure in place because having any organizational structure without a lead person is like having a body try to walk with its head cut off. We know that is impossible because one of the main functions that a head provides to the body is balance. It is the stabilizing factor for the other members. The things of God also require that a head be in place to execute the activities of ministry in excellence.

"...Christ is the head of the church; and He is the Savior of the body."
(Ephesians 5:23 NKJV)

As a leader, you must not be intimidated by a person's skill, or his ability, knowledge, level of expertise, or aptitude.

"And Chenaniah, chief of the Levites, was for song: he instructed about the song, because he was skillful."
(1 Chronicles 15:22)

We have come to terms with the fact that we fall in love with the heart of people, which sometimes makes it difficult to deal with the issue of their skill level. By the same token, too much focus on skill levels can be tricky because skill can also

77

cause us to build an entire segment of our worship activities around people who are extremely gifted or talented. Believe me when I tell you that is a set up for disaster. Liken what you are doing with the music ministry to the activities associated with building a house. Yet in this case, the foundation of the house must always be Christ.

"Except the LORD build the house, they labour in vain that build it: except the LORD keep the city, the watch man waketh but in vain."

(Psalm 127:1)

This leadership position of overseer has different titles attached to it depending on who asks you to fulfill the role and what you are asked to do. In some cases, different functions warrant different titles, but in some situations, the same function is given a different title; the determination of the title is at the discretion of the leadership. The titles can be Minister of Music, Music Pastor, Choir Director, Music Director, Worship Leader, Worship Pastor, Music Administrator and I've even heard the term Chief Levite. Now, some of these positions can co-exist depending on their function. However, the title is not as important as determining who will bear the responsibility of overseeing the functions and duties to be carried out in the department. Also, who will be the person everyone looks to musically on the platform should an issue arise? Someone must be in charge.

This section is dedicated to helping you develop tools that can be implemented immediately to provide additional structure to your music ministry. Each component should be written down and kept in a binder specifically labeled "Processes." Remember when you write things down you are actually giving life to them: *"Write the vision..."* (Habakkuk 2:2)

Purpose/Job Descriptions/Expectations

When you write out a person's purpose, you are telling them his or her reason for being in the music ministry.

Identifying his/her job description gives them guidelines for what they are to do. And when expectations are consummated, there is a clear understanding of the level of growth and service that is going to be expected from the individual. If you are currently a Minister of Music and do not have a job description, I would strongly encourage you to immediately go to the pastor and request one. It is imperative. You have to know what is required of you and what your established level of authority is. Trust me, it will help you in the future.

Qualifications

Qualifications spell out the qualities or "skill sets" that a person needs to operate effectively in a given area. A candidate should sufficiently prove themselves in each of the following areas in order for you to consider them for any position as a member of the choir or praise team, worship leader, or musician, etc.. You must evaluate the qualifications on some level before you can even make an accurate spiritual decision.

Musical Aptitude

Does the individual possess the musical skills and aptitude needed to be a positive addition to the music ministry? What level of skill/competence are you looking for? There are varying levels of skill, but keep in mind that there should be at least a basic proficiency level that all involved in the music ministry should have.

Spiritual Maturity

The spiritual maturity of the individual must be at a certain level for them to occupy a ministry position, whether it is a leadership or supporting role, within the congregation. Therefore, analyzing the spiritual qualifications of an individual includes observing their attitude, lifestyle, conduct, faithfulness, and their commitment to church and, ultimately, to God. Remember that the essence of worship is rooted in a relationship; there must be a relationship with the Father.

Administrative Agility

When seeking someone to fulfill a position of <u>leadership</u>, another key question to pose is related to their ability to organize and facilitate the "housekeeping" items for the position they will hold. To determine whether or not this is an area that needs to be developed, you might ask them to assist you in an administrative support role. The ability to handle administrative functions is crucial because where there is no order, there is chaos.

Leadership Ability

Yes, she is gifted and talented musically, but will people follow her? Some people are innately born to lead. That is somewhat obvious in many cases. When deciding if someone can handle a leadership position, focus on whether or not they are ready to lead instead of whether or not they are meant to lead. Can they effectively mobilize, manage, and motivate others to accomplish a goal? There are other traits you may wish to consider in reference to leadership abilities, including confidence, competence, and charisma.

For each of these areas, you must use some type of evaluation to gauge whether this person will be a fit for your ministry needs. You should define some criteria that can help you determine with some degree of accuracy whether or not this person's skills are compatible with your level of need.

Selection Process/Auditions/Entrance Requirements

The selection process is one that must be outlined and approved by the leadership when the final criteria are established. However, you must determine what it is you need to make the music department excel and continue to grow. There may be gifts that you can identify right within your prospective congregations. You should also be sensitive to the times when you may not need any additional talents in a particular area at the moment. For example, you may have ten altos, four sopranos, and nine tenors. When you hold an audition, you discover you have seven more altos and three more tenors in the congregation. If you bring on the new altos and tenors, you may cause the scale to be so imbalanced that it tips over and breaks everybody's neck, and that is not the result you want.

The selection process must include a level of discipline; you should not just take whatever you have at the time. Know what you need versus what you are able to use. Perhaps there has to be a waiting list, or maybe you need to shift parts around so that you can maintain or achieve balance.

Band Rotation/Structure

This will not apply to everyone, but if you have enough musicians for a rotation schedule, then use everyone by giving them an opportunity to express their talents and skills; this will automatically add a uniqueness to the worship service. When there are different musicians who are committed to the excellence of worship, they will each have their own God-given gift and personality that can be heard distinctly through the instruments as they play. This variety is wonderful, and you will want to make sure you use it.

When you are looking at the structure of any area of the music ministry, make certain that you have mapped out some organizational table that gives you an idea of who is doing what and when. This table can be an effective guide when it is prepared properly.

The list below offers a suggested format for the layout of the organizational components that you need to establish in order for your music ministry to flow at an optimum level. We'll move just a little further into each area of administration in the next chapter. Review and reflect on each of these areas, keeping in mind that all of the areas here may not apply to your particular situation. However, as you analyze and think through these areas, I am certain that they will stimulate your creativity, and fresh ideas for the music ministry of which you are a part will be revealed to you. Ultimately, you will begin to see increased synergy within the music ministry when you coordinate the components God has made available to you.

The following outline should be used to collectively pull together the adminstrative and spiritually practical aspects of the music ministry. This is an at-a-glance look at the areas diverse components of the music ministry. Once completed these items can yield invaluable information that can assist you in navigating each area of music ministry with clarity.

Minister of Music/Music Pastor
- Purpose/Job Description/Expectations
    Write It Out
- Qualifications
    Musical Aptitude
    Spiritual Maturity
    Administrative Agility
    Leadership Ability
- Selection Process
- Submission Factor

Musicians
- Purpose/Job Description/Expectations
    Write It Out
- Qualifications
    Musically Qualified (Style)
    Spiritually Qualified
- Selection Process/Auditions/Entrance Requirements
    What you need vs. what you can effectively use
- Band Rotation/Structure

Praise Leader/Teams
- Purpose/Job Descriptions/Expectations
    Write It Out
- Qualifications
    Spiritually Qualified (*Worship Qualifications are Unique*)
    Musically Qualified

- Selection Process/Auditions/Entrance Requirements
- Structure

Choir(s)

- Purpose/Job Description/Expectations
    Write It Out
- Qualifications
    Spiritually Qualified
    Musically Qualified
- Selection Process/Auditions/Entrance Requirements
    1. Main Adult Choir
    2. Youth Choir
    3. Children's Choir
    4. Male Chorus/Women's Chorus/Senior Choir/ Etc.
        How Many In Each Group
        When Do They Sing/Rehearse
        Enough Personnel for Effective Oversight/ Viability

Audio/Visual (Sound)

- Purpose/Job Description/Expectations
    Write It Out
- Qualifications
    Spiritually Qualified
    Technically Qualified
- Selection Process/Entrance Requirements

11

Getting Things in Perfect Harmony

In this chapter, we will continue to organize and develop an administrative rhythm to the aspects of music ministry. As indicated in the previous chapter, the more organized you are and the more tools you have developed to assist in facilitating an efficient music ministry, the easier the process of ministry will be for all involved. Therefore, let us delve further into the area of organizing and administrating.

Organizational Flow Chart

In any business, the organizational flow chart is a simple sketch that illustrates who reports to whom and what each person's function is under a particular supervisor or manager. From a practical standpoint, it should be a written description and a pictorial chart for quick viewing and assessment.

For example, in this case, the person who has overall oversight for the organization (Pastor) is on the first level, and the person who is assigned the overall position of control (Minister of Music) for the music ministry is on the next level. The next tier of leadership might include the Choir Director, Praise Team Leader, Band Leader, and the Sound Manager. In a pictorial view, that set up would look something like this:

As you can see, you have begun to detail your organizational structure. In an ideal scenario, each person's name and title should appear on the chart. An organizational chart can be an effective tool for not only identifying the reporting structure, but also illustrating the flow of communication within an organization. It can help build unity and improve efficiency by providing staff with a clear view of the chain of command that must be followed when addressing issues and challenges. Other tiers of leadership may include the assistant minister of music, section leaders, administrative assistants, dance team, children, youth, drama, and other officers.

Music Ministry Leadership Team

When a corporation is established, the second issue addressed after the name is determined is the selection of officers. Why might it be necessary to have officers within a music ministry? The reason might seem too acutely simple, but the fact is they provide an additional level of accountability and proficiency because the more specific responsibilities an individual has, the more focused, detailed, and effective that person can be at completing assigned tasks.

For example, the treasurer has specific tasks associated with the finances of the music ministry; therefore, the choir director is not worried about finances. He or she can concentrate on the selection of songs and should not be distracted by another list of responsibilities. Having a leadership team inside of the music ministry leads to increased opportunities for teamwork and collaboration.

I must not fail to address the obvious. Every music ministry will not have the resources needed to have separate individuals handling each of these areas exclusively. With that in mind, there is one piece of advice I recommend: use what you have. Don't try to do more than you are effectively capable of managing. Don't overwork those already on your team. That being said, continue to write the vision and put systems in place. Remind the people that although you may not be where you want to be right now, this is where we all are going!

Business Meetings

As much as is practical and warranted, try to keep business discussions to a minimum during rehearsals and conduct major business during specific business meetings. This demonstrates that you respect the time of the individuals who attend rehearsals; you must be sensitive to their time. I have also discovered that business meetings and rehearsals are much more productive when you keep them separate.

Budgets

You should prepare a budget at the beginning of every year and submit it to the leadership. I know some of you are wondering why because you think you aren't going to get it anyway! You should still compile one because it demonstrates vision, focus, and organization on your part. Your pastor will appreciate it even if he can't fulfill your request at the time. Then, one of the first questions that you should answer is how the money is gong to be acquired for the budget. Simply put, where is the money coming from? Will the music department be responsible for raising the funds needed independently from the church budget? Will the department need to supplement the funds allocated to it from the church, or will the church fund all the activities and needs associated with the music department completely?

Whether you receive partial or complete funding from the church budget, there will still need to be some concrete amount that the music department will have available to them. The leadership of the music department should be aware of this figure and respect the boundaries set by this budget unless alternate plans are in place to raise additional funding as needed.

Finally, itemizing the expenses of the music ministry will give you a good idea of where the ministry is financially and what items need to be covered and how often. For example, new music, equipment, staff, training, robe cleaning and other professional services are some of the items that need to be considered.

Yearly Goals *(Short Term/Long Term)*

Written goals are absolutely imperative for your ministry to make actual progress. This is especially true for the progression and growth of a music ministry. Everyone in the music ministry should be able to articulate the goals for the coming year. This allows them to internalize the vision and pray for its success. Make sure to differentiate between short term and long-term goals. These might include items like annual concerts, album recording, Christmas and Easter musicals, choir trips or fellowships, choir robes, and workshops. Anything that will require planning and execution—including the funding needed to accomplish these goals— should be added to your list.

Rules/Guidelines *(Governing Document)*

This document that outlines the rules and guidelines of the music department should incorporate the spirit and doctrinal beliefs of the church. So make sure the rules and guidelines are discussed with the pastor prior to implementation. Some of the items that must be addressed in this document are entrance requirements, attendance, attire, tardiness, rehearsals, engagements, vacations, leaves of absences, etc.

Anything that you want to clearly communicate to the members of the music department should be addressed in this document. Remember, members will not know what is expected of them if those expectations are not made known to them. You should also pay special attention to issues that pertain to conduct. The mission and purpose should also be reiterated in writing here. You should clearly articulate why you do what you do.

Administrative Forms

I know what you're thinking—more paperwork? Unfortunately, yes. I know that many people may not have the patience for handling and keeping track of forms and details required for managing these items. I suggest that someone, preferably someone with an aptitude for administration and organization, be assigned to complete these tasks. If you are a member of the music ministry at your church and have an ability to handle this responsibility, why not consider using your gift of administration in this manner? Just think of how your contribution will help take the music ministry to another level of efficiency.

Below is a list of just a few of the forms that I recommend be utilized in the music ministry. They have proven over the years to be quite necessary, as God has continued to develop my career and ministry in the area of music production and ministry facilitation.

1.) Music Ministry Application
2.) Notification of Change Form
        Leaves of Absences
        Vacations
        Change of Address/Status
3.) Audition Forms
4.) Music Logs
        Categorized List of Songs
        Authors
        Keys
        When Last Sung
5.) Equipment Logs
        Date of Purchase
        Serial Numbers
        Insurance/Warranty Information
        Date of Last Maintenance
        Photographs

The primary goal of this chapter was to share some tools that will help you better manage the components that are involved with music ministry. If you are in a support role, look at some of the other components listed above and begin to pray whether God would have you to become involved with another aspect above and beyond the position you are holding right now.

I can attest to the benefits of this kind of organization; once the music ministry makes the adjustments and becomes comfortable with the processes, you will begin to soar to greater heights in ministry for Him.

12

Build It Up!

As the music department continues to grow, you will want to make sure a healthy ministry environment is being maintained. Trust and mutual respect must be cultivated in this environment to breed unity and provide a wonderful haven in which the presence of the Lord can dwell.

Pastoral/Minister of Music Relationship

The success for this kind of healthy model should be seen most readily in the relationship between the Pastor and the Minister of Music. It is one of the most critical, yet sometimes one of the most contentious, relationships in the church. However, the truth is, it was never intended to be that way. I suppose I should park here for just a moment. Even though I am a national recording artist, producer, and songwriter, for the purposes of our discussion here, it is probably most important to note that I'm the son of a pastor (or a PK—preacher's kid—as we are sometimes known), and I grew up in the church. I know what it's like to be the only musician at a church and what it's like to work with a full orchestra. I know what it's like to be the minister of music for a church with 50 members and for a church with 12,000 members. I know what it's like to have to play on an out of tune piano that has brown keys because all the ivory has chipped off and what it's like to play with state-of-the-art equipment. I know what it's like to be paid and not to be paid. I also know what it's like to conceitedly sit on the organ feeling like I was in control of the service regardless of what the pastor said, and I know what it's like to sit on the organ and be publicly humiliated by a pastor in front of the congregation. Why am I saying all this? To indicate that I've been around enough to most certainly

> Trust and mutual respect must be cultivated

know a healthy Pastoral/Minister of Music relationship from a poor one and the impact that relationship—good or bad—can have on a ministry.

I've seen possessive, controlling pastors use and then literally crush the spirits of many musicians, leaving them wounded and bleeding on the side of the road. I've also seen ego-driven, self-absorbed musicians literally holding churches hostage with their gifts. I have witnessed how contentious Pastoral/Minister of Music relationships literally split churches. Likewise, I've experienced the incredible power, growth, and success found in a healthy (though not perfect) relationship. This might be a good point at which to go back and review chapter one again.

Communication is key in any relationship, particularly this one. Make sure you both are in a position of reciprocal impartation. As the Minister of Music, make sure you are capturing the pastor's vision and sharing your vision for the music ministry. As the pastor, make sure you are covering, nurturing, and resisting the urge to micro-manage. This is also the time to establish boundaries of authority. The Minister of Music must know when his or her authority ends and the pastor's begins when difficult situations arise or decisions must be made. For example, does the Minister of Music have the authority to relieve someone of his or her duties in the music ministry? Can he or she order needed supplies without prior consent?

Communication is key in any relationship.

When these boundaries are set, make sure those in leadership and supporting positions in the music ministry respect them. If you are in the choir or on the praise team, make sure you are aware of where the authoritative lines are drawn. It is imperative for you to function with excellence and submission, so do not be afraid to ask questions pertaining to authority; you would not want to handle situations inappropriately because it can cause division unnecessarily. If something does arise and you are not sure with whom you should address a particular situation, go to the Minister of Music because he or she should be able to steer you in the right direction.

Naturally, a spiritual connection will take place, and it will be visible on the platform during services. When you develop a spiritually healthy bond between the ministries of the church, you are able to select songs that complement the goals of the ministry, and the comfort that has been established will certainly make the pastor feel as if you welcome his input when he is feeling led in a particular direction with the music. It's about trust.

If you are sensitive to the move of the Holy Spirit, you will be on one accord with the pastor during a service. This should be your goal. In addition, make sure you make some contact with the pastor prior to service if possible. This is an excellent time to pray together and make sure you are on target for the mandate of that service.

Planning & Preparation

Planning and preparation are crucial. You should plan your rehearsals, services, and meetings. Each of these areas requires prior thought and attention. When these areas are planned prior to the actual meeting, you will see phenomenal results with regard to the transitioning through each subject or song. You maximize the use of the time allocated to your ministry, and you are able to demonstrate your respect for the people in attendance by giving them the opportunity to leave on time, which will cause them to embrace your requests for future meetings, rehearsals, engagements, or other activities.

Your rehearsals are time to do just that—to practice what will be done in the next service. Therefore, making sure you are prepared with the material that needs to be perfected is the overall goal here. In addition, rehearsals should also be a time of worship—not just work! We will discuss this in more detail later.

Occasionally including the pastor in rehearsals is an excellent way to bring a stronger sense of purpose to the overall scheme of things. This is not just a dutiful obligation; it is a service and expression of worship unto the Lord. Sometimes, the pastor's presence may bring that aspect of centering into a rehearsal.

The same principles apply when it comes to planning services and meetings. Make sure you establish a sense of purpose in each meeting and service. Service preparation should be handled deliberately and carefully. Prior preparation should be evident by the seamless flow of the music during the service.

Music preparation is a large part of getting ready for service because it encompasses the selection of music that is not only in line with the spiritual climate of the church, but it must also be appropriate for the group that is available to the ministry at that time. Taking the time to prepare allows you and others to give your best to the Lord in whatever capacity you are functioning in at any given moment.

Investment

There is no simple way to say the obvious. You must invest time, finances, talent, and other resources in order to obtain a maximum return from the music ministry as a whole. Some personnel may require a salary allocation. I know this may be a controversial concept to some, but it is a biblical reality nonetheless. You may also need some talents that may not already be available to you in your local congregation. You might have to seek outside resources to acquire what you need.

Continuous investment must also be made into the individuals you currently have giving their service to the ministry. These individuals should be offered additional training and opportunities to develop their gifts as well. Sometimes when additional training opportunities are offered, you will discover additional talent resources that were undeveloped, but are useful to the furtherance of the ministry.

Logically, you might need to purchase and maintain some equipment. Therefore, it is wise to develop a budget to handle such situations if and when they occur. It has been said that you can determine a ministry's priorities are by looking at where its money is spent.

Effective Leadership

Although we have spent a great deal of time discussing leadership, I would like to provide a reminder here. Remember to reproduce yourself so that you don't limit the effectiveness of the music ministry. Mentorship is very important in this area of ministry reproduction. You must be willing to take time to share your knowledge and gifts with others to benefit them and your ministry. This process of reproduction will help the ministry continue to thrive long after you hold a position of leadership because you never know where God intends to send you or how He plans to use you.

The ability to delegate effectively goes hand in hand with reproducing yourself. Delegation is often abused; you need a great deal of spiritual sensitivity to master it and produce great results. Many people have difficulty learning this important skill; some people burn themselves out trying to do everything and be everything, and this really limits their level of effectiveness as leaders.

The spiritual sensitivity that is required in delegation is the same reflection that should be seen in everything that you do. The balance and sensitivity to the Spirit is something that must be developed and refined with time—time spent in the presence of the Father. Knowing His direction for the music ministry and having a close intimate

Mentorship is very important in this area of ministry reproduction.

relationship with Him, places you in a position to walk in a continued, daily sensitivity to His will.

Last, as a leader, you should always strive to build a team atmosphere, give spiritual impartation, and exhibit the behaviors and attitudes you want others to emulate! Never expect more of others than you are willing to give yourself, and never neglect to surround yourself with people who know more than you do about a particular area. In order to do this, you must know what it is that you don't know. In order to know what you don't know, you will have to look inward and take an honest evaluation of yourself. By nature, we hate to do self-evaluations, but the best leaders realize this self-assessment and adjustment is vital to growth; developing a life of balance is imperative if you plan to prosper.

At this point, let's jump into the boat of self-development. I know this may not be the most exciting destination on our journey, but let's take the time to observe the beauty of living a life of balance that includes practically taking care of our temple. Open your ears to hear the level of clarity, emotional stability, and stamina you will need to possess as you take a moment to manage the element most important to the Father above and beyond the music or the ministry—YOU!

13

The Rest Is Up to YOU!

Many times, individuals who have a gift for music or operate in some capacity thereof usually have a predisposition to correlate things in life with the rhythm of music. Because of the subject matter of this book, I am compelled to speak to you about subjects that relate to practical applications for effective musicianship. However, these are items that do not deal with the music ministry directly, but if mastered, they can have an impact on it. Why, because, these items deal with you.

As we stroll through this chapter, we are going to take the time to address practical lifestyle issues that affect everything else you do within the ministry of music. You must realize that if your lives are out of balance, there is no way you can belt out a straight tune.

Prayer

I like to start with the foundation of prayer. *"And He spake a parable unto them to this end, that men ought always to pray and not to faint" (Luke 18:1 KJV)*. This scripture is very, very clear. There is never a time when you should not pray. There is never a thing that you should not pray about. Prayer is of primary importance to God and should, therefore, be of primary importance to you, the believer.

It is impossible to balance the scale of life without a consistent, sincere prayer life. There is just no way to move into anything without a focused, dedicated line of communication with the Father. How else will you know what to do, what chord to play, or what song to sing? How else can you give your petitions to Him unless you communicate with Him yourself? You cannot pass a note to someone in class and have them pass the note to the person you want to read it. That does not work with God. That is not how He operates. You must come to Him yourself because open, two-way communication with God is the basis for prayer.

"Prayer is not a performance, but, simply coming to God with a sincere heart...acknowledging who He is by sharing my situations, making my requests known and listening for Him to speak."

-*Lilly Lester*
The Prayer Habit

Every person in the music ministry must spend time developing the area of prayer. God is your source of inspiration and insight. Otherwise, the music is pointless. If there is no relationship, there is no worship. How can you worship a God you don't know? How can you say you have a melody in your heart for God or that you want to sing or play a song for Him and you won't even talk to Him? I know He loves the singing, but He also loves to hear your everyday struggles, desires, disappointments, and questions. God is ultimately seeking a relationship with you. After all, He is a Father with an intimate heart waiting for you to pull up a chair and chat with Him.

Rest

The simplest thing I can say about rest is—get it. One way or another, make sure you get adequate rest. I can stand in defense of the musicians, artists, and other personnel that function in music ministry full-time. When ministry is your career, you can get trapped in the functions that are required to live. It is the easiest thing in the world to go days on very few hours of sleep. It is hard to find the button that disconnects you from your life of work, but subconsciously, you know you should take the time to get adequate rest for your body, mind, and spirit.

Doctors will tell you that rest—in addition to the consumption of eight to 10 glasses of water a day—is the most important thing for your body. You are aware of the fact that rest repairs and balances your functions; it also helps your body build up your immune system so that it can fight disease if and when it tries to enter. Keep in mind that rest is not always sleep. It may just be sitting down to read a book or holding a simple conversation with a loved one. Rest encompasses quiet activity with little or no motion. In layman's terms, it means to stop working—physically and mentally.

From a vocal standpoint, I know you've probably been told at least a dozen different things to do and take to help your voice: hot tea, lemon and honey, zinc lozenges, Throat Coat®, salt water gargles, humidifiers, etc. These all have their place, but the best thing for your voice is actually REST! Yes, just stop talking. When you have to speak, learn to speak defensively. Give only what you know your voice can comfortably give. Always be careful to balance your "voice use time" with your "voice recovery time" (silence).

I know, I know. We all can say, "It's one thing to know this and yet another to do it." I agree. But in order for you to function at your optimum level, you must know your limitations. The threshold of burden should be managed properly so that you will live longer and better with many more years to enjoy the gifts of family and friends and to continue to advance the kingdom of God by continuing to participate in lifting a pure sound of worship from the earth to Him.

The simple truth is if you don't voluntarily give your body the rest it needs, believe me, it will *take it*. And, when it takes the rest, you will be on the verge of a complete shut down, which always happens at the most inopportune times. Take my advice and *give* your body what it needs.

> *Make sure you get adequate rest.*

Diet & Exercise

STOP! Don't turn the page here. I know you hate to hear these two words in the same sentence together. Listen, I know you know the statistics pertaining to heart disease, high-blood pressure, cholesterol, and diabetes. I am on your side. I am not a spokesman for any medical organization or salesperson trying to get you to purchase a three-year membership at a neighborhood gym that you are not going to use. But hear me out.

I am coming from a very simple position. If you watch what you put in your body, you will get better mileage out of it, and you will be able to do what you do better. No, I am not suggesting that you only eat rice cakes and water, but you should make some changes in concert with your doctor's recommendations that will benefit your overall health. For example, vitamins can be a simple addition to your current regimen that will make a difference in your overall health. Make a small change today, consult with your physician, and you will feel better for it!

> *Balance your "voice use time" with your "voice recovery time" (silence).*

Next, as far as exercise goes...I know—who has time? It's such a pain to get started, but the benefits outweigh the inconveniences. How are you going to be able to continue to lead worship for three or four services, and additional rehearsals every week? How are you going to handle a three hour concert, live recording, or a 20 city bus tour? It takes stamina, strength, and endurance. Fitness experts agree that aerobic exercise, that is, exercise that develops heart-lung strength and endurance (e.g., walking, jogging, swimming, bicycling), is the most important form of exercise for maintaining and maximizing your health. You can make a change as simple as walking for 20 minutes a day three times a week. Remember that you are your instrument; whatever improves the instrument also helps your voice. Believe it or not, singing is an athletic activity. You will get better performance from your voice if you exercise. I'm not an expert, but I hear you'll feel better, too.

Proper Breathing & Posture

Once you start exercising, you will be better able to

master the breathing techniques set forth for you by your section or choir leaders.

"Breath is the foundation on which singing is established, and good breathing is the basis for all good singing. It furnishes the energy for phonation, resonance, and articulation. Without respiration, none of the other elements of singing would function."

-Richard Alderson
Complete Handbook of Voice Training

Yes, you might have a great pair of lungs, but if you are slouched over while you're singing, you are not properly preparing or supporting your vocals chords for singing. You are obstructing the windpipe and restricting the wind flow. This is how some people experience vocal strain. They are not using the proper breathing or posture mechanisms for singing. Musicians should also practice proper posture when they are playing. Make sure your back is straight when you sing or play.

Using proper breathing techniques and posture when you sing is fundamental to sustaining tone and sound. This will improve your sound quality and add value to your music ministry. Remember, a perfected sound of worship is always music to the Lord's ears!

Environment

I wanted to talk about environment because I have found that knowing what is going on around me can prove lethal if I am unaware and quite profitable when I am aware. The goal here should be to observe and analyze your surroundings. For instance, before you are about to sing, check to make sure that no one around you is smoking. This is not a sermon on the Biblical mandate for or against smoking. For the purpose of this book, we are sticking with the facts concerning the affects smoking has on your vocal chords and lungs, which can instantly make it more difficult for you to sing.

In addition, the weather is another major component to consider, especially when you are in an unfamiliar climate. Check things like the pollen and humidity levels. Is it going to rain? How cold is it going to be?

We can also look at environment from another perspective, one which provides a more practical appeal from the music ministry standpoint. When you enter a church that you are not familiar with, the environment plays a substantial role in how well your effort to minister will be fulfilled. When you enter the facility or church, there are things that you should notice from a technical standpoint.

You should check microphones and sound equipment to make sure everything is functioning properly. What are the instruments like? Is the piano tuned? Do you need to bring your own drums? Is the church too hot or cold? Something as simple as making sure

Using proper breathing techniques and posture when you sing is fundamental to sustaining tone and sound.

you know the theme and vision of the church in which you will minister when you have been invited to fellowship in another arena outside your particular congregation, will have a tremendous impact.

Whatever you do, be flexible so that you can adapt to the atmosphere and environment in which you find yourself. Be careful not to complain. Be flexible and adjust, but do your homework! It is the ministry we give which is of supreme importance. Do what you can and flow with the environment.

Each of the above items represents something that will enhance your ability to serve in the music ministry and respect the temple of God with more awareness. You should strive to offer your best in your life to the Lord while on stage and when you are away from the stage, the pulpit, and audiences. I pray that these additional motivators will help you in your ministry to Him.

Now, let's get back on the horse, grab the reins, and gallop to the next pit stop. Is there peace on your platform?

14

Peace In the House

Peace

The absence of war or other hostilities; freedom from quarrels and disagreement; harmony.

The first question that comes to mind where after reading this definition and trying to relate it to the music ministry is, "Are there really hostilities, quarrels, and disagreements in the music department?" This is a naïve question with a simple answer: yes. There are many common human responses to situations and circumstances; with any ministry in the church or in a more practical sense, whenever you get more than three people together, agreement becomes a real task.

We should accept, and even embrace, the fact that, at times, there will be differences of opinion (yes, conflict) in the ministry. Such is the nature of people, whether they are family or congregation members, business associates, or neighborhood softball league buddies. When you attend church, you experience diverse cultures, backgrounds, denominations, personalities and experiences; your goal is to try and form a cohesive unit. When done successfully, it is a fundamentally powerful representation of God's Kingdom. However, if this representation is not managed effectively, it can also be fertile ground for conflict. The challenge before us remains how to manage the conflict in a way that engenders growth and minimizes chaos.

The Unified Front

Though managing a unified group of individuals is a challenging undertaking, it is not impossible. In previous chapters, we discussed a variety of tools, topics, and techniques that can help you establish a harmonious presence in the music ministry.

One of the first things you should examine is the relationship between the leader of the music department/ministry and the pastor of the church. We discussed this earlier but it bears repeating. The anointing flows from the head down. The same is true with regard to the tone of order and peaceful relations in the ministry. In this case, specifically within the music ministry, I cannot stress how important and sensitively imperative this relationship is to the flow of music ministry. In many cases, I have found that it makes the difference between just a "good" music scenario and an extremely successful one.

"Don't take everything personally."

Without question, unity is a key factor. Not only should the leadership build a sense of unity, but a level of unity must also exist among the staff in the music department as well. I have found the best way to build unity within a music department is through occasional social fellowship away from the church. This outside fellowship time should not be limited to only one sector of the music ministry. It should encompass all participants: musicians, sound personnel, choir members, praise team, a projectionist—anyone who is actively involved in the worship ministry during services. When members of the group spend time together, they learn more about one another and increase opportunities to pray for one another. Before you know it, they form stronger relationships, and the more harmonious the environment, the less conflict there will be.

It takes everyone working together to bring about an excellent level of praise and worship to the congregation. Therefore, when the time for fellowship and apprecation comes, everyone who makes the ministry flow properly should also be involved. Being creative with the fellowship times should always be a goal. Taking suggestions from the members of the music department will also ensure that you are tapping into their needs and desires as a group. For example, one time our music department hosted a "Parent's Night Out." My staff and I watched the children at church while the parents had time away from the children to themselves. Parents needed and appreciated the few hours of free time and the fact that we would think enough of them to do such a thing. The goal is to be creative; God will undoubtedly give you an ingenious plan for the group in which you are involved.

Star Struck

By developing solid, sincere relationships, you stand a greater chance of avoiding a barrage of star struck saints. They will come. You may be leading them or sitting next to them in the choir stand right now. Rest assured, they are all over the church. You can spot the star struck saints easily because they will treat worship service like an episode of "American Idol!" They carry a sense about them that says, "There is no worship unless I lead it," or "Worship does not start until I arrive." Yuck.

They generally defy any rules set before them and feel that rehearsal is a waste of time, simply because they are so gifted. Sadly, some of the "monsters" you have on your teams are ones you created! You must be careful to make sure that no one is allowed to become (or to think they have become) bigger than the worship. Also resist the temptation to build your ministry around someone's talent because that's a sure set-up for disaster! Make sure the foundation and focus always remains Christ. One method I have used is to teach the lead part of a song to two or three different people right from the beginning. This prevents anyone from saying it's "their" song and minimizes the "star" effect, which then keeps us on the road of peace within the ministry.

The Basic Truth

In previous chapters, we discussed things like structure, which is simply making sure you know the rules, order, and expectations of the music ministry, and communication, which is important because you need to make sure everyone understands and follows established expectations. If you are a member of the music ministry and do not hold a position of leadership in that ministry, I encourage you to ask questions because what you don't know should be available and explained to you with clarity.

I am sure that at this point, you are concretely secure in the need for investment in training, personnel, and equipment and understand that these items alone cannot replace the selection processes needed to acquire the right personnel for your particular organization. In addition, preparation (rehearsal) is another critical component you must consider when trying to develop and/or maintain an environment of peace within the music ministry. I am an advocate for rehearsal being a time of more than music preparation; it should also be a time of fellowship and team building, and we will discuss this in greater detail in the next chapter.

> *It takes everyone working together to bring about an excellent level of praise and worship to the congregation*

Where Do We Go From Here?

Another sure—fire way to kill a platform of peace is to neglect to know where the music ministry is going. This, my friend, is a disaster waiting to happen. Having a clear focus for where the ministry is going is very important. I believe that you should know what you currently have at your disposal. Utilizing those resources to the best of your ability and visualizing something greater continues to push you toward progress and excellence.

As you implement something new from your written plan (Habakkuk 2:2), survey the congregation and the members of the music department. This will help you gauge the responses to a new initiative; in addition, it fosters a sense of belonging to the congregation and the music ministry as well.

The underlying goal is to eradicate complacency because complacency is a breeding ground for complaining, which is an enemy of peace.

Put On Your Heavy Coat

We all know that when it gets cold, we must bring out our heavier outerwear. If we don't, we will feel like the wind is blowing straight through to our bones. It is not a comfortable feeling. Sometimes our communication with others reminds us of this bitterly cold experience. Miscommunication or improper communication can leave a sting that may be chilling to your soul (the place of will, emotions, intellect, etc.); however, you should not always regard statements that are direct as mean or improper. In fact, you should analyze the timing and manner in which the comment or statement was made. Feedback can sometimes be difficult to stomach, but when given in the spirit of helpfulness, this type of constructive criticism can help you improve, learn, and grow.

A friend recently told me that he felt that I was mean and indifferent because I didn't use a lot of words to answer his questions. That was just not the case. My personality is calm and congenial, but I don't waste words.

I shared this with you to say, "Don't take everything personally." Just because someone's comments aren't presented in a manner that you prefer does not mean that the remarks were meant to assault you. Do people say and do things that are inappropriate? Absolutely. But keep in mind that there are no perfect people or situations. This is why it is important to know that you are called to serve in particular area. You will need to have thick skin and a warm coat to make it through some chilling encounters, but when you know your purpose, you stay when you want to go. Your commitment will not necessarily be to a person, but to the "calling" and purpose that you and the Father have solidified in your heart. God placed you there for a reason. Just be willing to stick and stay!

Tackle Conflict Head-On

We have already determined that conflict will arise, so the issue is not *if*, but *when*. When conflict arises, it is crucial to promote and engage in open and honest dialogue. It is also essential to move swiftly to address any issues head on. Whatever you do, don't allow matters to just sit and fester. The longer you take to deal with things, the bigger the problem gets. Things like anger, frustration, unforgiveness, and secrecy pull their strength from a simple factor—time. The longer it sits, the bigger it gets.

Therefore, it is important to establish a comment/grievance policy that gives people a forum to voice their opinions. If individuals feel that their concerns are important and will be addressed fairly, they will more willing to share when a problem does arise. This will help minimize conflict.

Make sure communication is clear with the pastor as well, so that it is clear what issues should be handled internally and what issues require pastoral intervention. Just remember that just because two houses look alike does not mean they are made of the same material. The only real way to find out what a house is made of is by how well it weathers a storm. If you manage conflict effectively, you and your team will grow. Your tree will grow higher and your roots deeper.

"He shall be like a tree planted by the rivers of water, that brings forth its fruit in its season. Whose leaf also shall not wither; and whatsoever he does shall prosper." *(Psalm 1:3 NKJV)*

15

Practice Makes Perfect

Over the past decade, one of the components of music ministry that my name has become synonymous with is choirs. I have worked with choirs for many years and have held hundreds of choir rehearsals. Therefore, I felt it appropriate to dedicate a specific chapter to giving simple but vital information that I have acquired through much trial and error in order that choir members and music directors alike would have a blueprint of the core functions of the choir rehearsal. The tips that are provided are easy to incorporate into your music ministry. I have purposely tried to keep the information generic in tone for that reason. After you have digested this information, I hope you will return to your music ministry with a renewed sense of determination and dedication because when you give your all in rehearsal, you are giving your all to God.

Give It All You've Got!

Ideally, rehearsals should be a time of preparation and study for the singers and musicians for the purpose of perfecting the musical and vocal gifts used in the service of the Lord. Often times, however, rehearsals become a social occasion where little, if any, meaningful work is accomplished.

The purpose of rehearsals is *"to enhance, improve, and enlarge skills for service within the music ministry."* Rehearsals should be one of the highlights of the week for those who participate in the music ministry. They should be stimulating, exciting, innovative, and creative. The members should be glad they came because they are participating in something that is well planned, interesting, and fast-paced. This time should never be boring and should be utilized strategically also as a time for pouring back into the membership of musicians and singers.

"Study to shew thyself approved unto God, a workmen that needth not be ashamed, rightly dividing the word of truth."   (2 Timothy 2:15)

If this scripture applies to pastors, ministers, and the like, it most certainly applies to the music ministry. Rehearsals are crucial to the development of an effective and powerful music ministry. You must remember that the anointing of God, which we should all seek and must possess, is not a substitute for preparation. There is no excuse for not putting in the time and dedication necessary for perfecting your praise to the Lord.

If you think about it, it is unfair to ask God to pour out His precious anointing on something that you know is "raggedy" and unprepared. How unfair indeed! This situation is no different than one in which a student asks God to help him pass a big test even though he has not made any effort to study and prepare himself. That student deserves to fail!

The bottom line is this: you must practice! Then watch the level of power and anointing that will explode when the Lord takes your practice and attaches His anointing. What a powerful combination waiting to explode. If you're not careful, your eyebrows could be singed!

Stand Up and Be Counted!

The responsibility for a successful, spiritual, and effective rehearsal rests primarily with the music minister/director. However, there is a significant level of responsibility assigned to the choir members as well. The music minister/director has a responsibility to prepare, provide, and promote an atmosphere conducive for musicians and choir members to function at their best. However, he or she is limited to actual execution of talent.

It is important to note at this point that, if at all possible, musicians should have separate rehearsals. The musicians should come to the choir's rehearsal prepared to execute the musical accompaniment at a level that allows the choir to be effective. However, the same principles and guidelines for commitment and dedication must apply to the musicians as well as the choir members. Now that could be another whole chapter.

Choir members should be faithful in their attendance and must take rehearsal time seriously. It goes without saying that things come up from time to time, but you should make sure your attendance is not a sporadic occurrence. Can you imagine how you bless the minister of music when you bring notebooks, bibles, and other material to each rehearsal to increase the efficiency and effectiveness of rehearsals. Members who come week after week, regular as clockwork, rain or shine, cold or hot, regardless of what is on TV...they are faithful to the rehearsal time designation. What an honor!

Believe me when I tell you I know how disheartening it is to prepare music and plan an exciting, innovative rehearsal only to have a handful of members in attendance. Of course, I am grateful for those who are in attendance, but it is extremely difficult to teach a song to half a choir one week and the other half of the choir another week. There are really no words to express the frustration felt when this happens.

When choir members realize that their commitment to the choir is a service to God, then it will put their heart in a position to be supportive and cooperative with the minister of music, musicians, and section leader(s). This is

> *Rehearsals should be stimulating, exciting, innovative, and creative.*

important on many different levels because everyone involved is depending on you to participate and do your part in the worship experience at each service. If you happen to disagree with a decision or request of someone in leadership, please respect the other members of the choir by expressing those grievances privately and not during the rehearsal time.

Having said that, I must reiterate the importance of having people come out for quality rehearsals—not something that was thrown together at the last minute. If the rehearsal time is a first-rate experience, people will want to come out to be a part of it. When a rehearsal offers something tangible to the people involved and is consistently stimulating, interesting, refreshing, innovative, challenging, exciting, spiritually beneficial, and on occasion, humorous, choir members will be encouraged to be punctual and to attend on a regular basis for fear that if they miss rehearsal, they might miss something exciting!

Note that the days of the Minister of Music/Director doing all the work are over! I require choir members to bring tape recorders to every rehearsal, so that they can take the tape and rehearse at home. Also, when there are a couple of songs I'm going to teach from a particular album, I request that all choir and band members purchase the album, and I tell them what songs I want them to learn and by what date. Yes, I know I'll probably have to correct some things, but we will be so much further along in the process. It will also mean that we're all taking responsibility for preparing new material.

Choir members should be faithful in their attendance and must take rehearsal time seriously.

If you are responsible for the task of enhancing rehearsals, below are a few foundational tips for increasing productivity and attendance:

1)   *Remember that the rehearsal time is a time of worship!*
Every rehearsal should begin with a period of praise and worship, prayer, and devotion. Take time to study the Word concerning the ministry of music at the beginning of each rehearsal. This will serve to further inspire and equip the choir and insure they develop a spiritual understanding that explains why they are doing what they do.

Also, be careful to keep the discussion about the business of the choir to a minimum before rehearsals. If something pressing needs to be discussed, convey it in a clear, concise, and direct manner. Call a separate meeting to discuss items that require extensive discussion.

2)   *As a leader, make sure you are prepared.*

Have an agenda, so that you will have a visual reference for what you want to accomplish and stick to it as much as the Lord will allow. Never waste the attendees' time by practicing on them because you are not sure of where you are going in rehearsal.

Make certain you are prepared to teach new material. You will lose the confidence and attention of the choir and congregation if you do not keep fresh material in front of them. This could be perceived as a sign of laziness.

Do not be afraid to practice! Keep going over something until it's right. But, by the same token, know when enough is enough and when it is time to move on to another piece of material.

3)   *Start on time - Every time.*

When members show up late, do not follow their lead. You must start on time. It is unfair to the members who come on time to be forced to wait for those who did not get there at the designated time. They are members ready to work, so get to work. There is no justifiable reason to wait.

I remember having an issue with people showing up on time to rehearsal. So, one rehearsal I had a bus waiting at the church at 7 p.m., our designated start time. I then gathered everyone that was there on time, put them on the bus, and took them all out to dinner. Those that came at their usual time (7:15 p.m. — 7:30 p.m.) were left behind. Well, that pretty much dealt with our timeliness issues from there on out! Be creative.

I would also suggest that you start the rehearsal with something familiar in a comfortable register for their voices so that they can warm up gently. This is acceptable and will allow stragglers to come in without missing a great deal of material. But at all costs, be on time!

4)   *Work fast and work hard.*

Keep rehearsals moving and keep the choir busy at all times. Do not allow time for whispering, jokes, or prolonged conversation. Make sure to mix things up for them. This will keep them on their toes and provide an element of excitement.

5)   *Occasionally, prepare times of fellowship (refreshments, tokens of appreciation, etc.).*

As I've indicated before, this will help build a cohesive team of people that feel connected to each other. Make sure this is done after rehearsal so that they can have an uninterrupted exchange and enjoy the freedom of the fellowship.

Although I only highlighted five tips here, rest assured that there are many other techniques and ways of doing things. The primary thing to remember is that rehearsals should be a focused, purposeful, and intense time of practice and preparation for your service to the Lord each week through music.

The leader must be prepared and organized, and the members must exhibit faithfulness, responsibility, and commitment. With this combination, you will never come up short in presenting a quality program that meets the needs of the people internally within the music department and externally within the congregation. I don't know about you, but that sounds like a win-win situation, and that should be music to your ears.

16

The Heart of the Matter

"Yet a time is coming and has now come when the true worshipers will worship the Father in spirit and truth, for they are the kind of worshipers the Father seeks. God is spirit, and his worshipers must worship in spirit and in truth." (John 4:23-24)

We have journeyed through many ministry principles, concepts, ideas and tools. By this point, you have hopefully gathered much practical information on the music ministry. I am delighted at the momentum we have built up to this point, but as we close this book, it is my heart's desire that if you don't get anything else from any other chapter in this book, know that this chapter is written from my heart to yours and is really the foundation upon which this book is written.

The thoughts outlined in this chapter serve a function similar to the aorta. The aorta is attached to your heart; one of its major functions is to supply blood and deliver nutrients to your heart. There are other veins, arteries, and capillaries that branch out from it, but it is the primary artery that sits in the middle of the body, playing a substantial role in regulating the successful function of our heart's health.

The same is true within the topic of fraudulent worshippers functioning in ministry. Yes, the chapters before this meant something. They were the veins, which replenish and cleanse and the arteries and capillaries that deliver the nutrients that allow the blood (knowledge and principles) to flow to the aorta artery (our relationship), so that the heart (church/music ministry) can function at its full potential. If the veins and arteries are blocked anywhere along the way, blood does not flow freely to the heart; this is one of the main culprits when an individual suffers a heart attack.

The same holds true for the church and music ministry. If the principles outlined in this chapter are not exercised, the blockage this will cause will ultimately result in an attack or breakdown. This is not necessary and is certainly not the will of God for us as His people.

"But be ye doers of the word, and not hearers only, deceiving your own selves."   *(James 1:22)*

The essence of this chapter can be wrapped up in one question: *"Are you a music ministry imposter?"*

Imposter - *One who deceives, defrauds, or cheats others by pretending to be what he is not; one that assumes false identity or title for the purpose of deception;* **Synonyms** - *pretender, fraud, phony, fake, counterfeit, artificial, imitator, impersonator, plastic, superficial, bogus, contrived, hypocrite, illegitimate...*

A few years ago, there was a game show called "To Tell The Truth." It began with three or four individuals on stage who all identified themselves as the same person. The object of the game was to answer a series of questions in order to eliminate the imposters and determine who was really telling the truth. Contestants could not select who was telling the truth just by looking at or hearing the participants because they all looked and sounded like they were telling the truth. In actuality, most of them were not who they claimed to be at all. They were imposters.

Our objective here is to investigate and expose what I would call *Fraudulent Worship*, or perhaps more accurately, *Fraudulent Worshippers*. Fraudulent worship takes place outside the scriptural pattern and mandate of *"...spirit and in truth,"* outlined in John 4. This worship is manufactured and made to look like it is genuine, but in reality, it is far from it. Let me make it clear that I am not necessarily embarking on the characteristics of *idol* worship (although we could probably spend quite a bit of time right there) because we all know that in Exodus 20:3, God commands that we should have no other gods before Him. However, the dialogue of this focus is on those of us in the "household of faith." Yes, even those of us who are worship leaders. This includes, and is not limited to, those who enter into the house of God week after week lift up their hands in the sanctuary and magnify, glorify, exalt, and praise the Lord, yet do not live the life of worshippers. They are double agents who look, sound, and act like worshippers, but they are imposters in disguise.

Before you jump in like an undercover agent trying to identify the imposters, you must first give yourself a self-evaluation. The ultimate goal is not solely about your trying to identify the impostors that may be around in your music ministry (although that may have its place in certain environments). The most significant issue is the consistent evaluation of your own lifestyle of worship. You must make sure that **you** are indeed worshipping in … "spirit and in truth!" This is not always an easy process to undergo. Just think how incredibly awful it would be to spend all the time you spend in church, or on some other platform, weekly going "through the motions" of worship, just to discover at the end that God never really knew you at all (Matt. 7:21-23).

Here is a little self-evaluation quiz. Only you know the answers. And only you know if you are an imposter.

1. *Do you get more excited about Sunday morning worship than Monday morning worship?*
2. *Do you miss rehearsal often except when it is your turn to sing lead or render a solo?*
3. *Is the behavior people see in the parking lot before service consistent with the behavior they see on the platform?*
4. *When you lead worship, does it seem like a solo performance?*
5. *Do you lead worship, but never really worship yourself?*
6. *Is praise what you do or who you are?*
7. *When was the last time you talked to God?*

8. *If you lead worship on Sunday and no one tells you what a great job you did, do you walk around depressed all week and threaten not to return?*

9. *Are you more concerned about your performance than His presence?*

If you answered yes to any of these questions, watch out because you might be the double agent. Here are 10 critical principles to consider as you evaluate how genuine and true your worship is:

1) *The true essence of worship is true relationship. No Real Relationship. No Real Worship.*

Where there is no true relationship with the Father, there can be no true worship of the Father. You must routinely check the state of your relationship with Him. If you're not careful, you'll find yourself just going through the motions, worshipping the Father out of duty or routine and not because of your real relationship. Believe me, I speak from experience. I have *been there, done that!* God demands and desires a true relationship. This is not an optional request. God is serious about His relationship with you on many levels; therefore, you must be as well. You should take the time to evaluate your worship by evaluating your relationship with God. The truth is, the closer you get to Him, the more meaningful, substantive, and genuine your worship becomes.

"He replied, 'Isaiah was right when he prophesied about you hypocrites; as it is written: 'These people honor me with their lips, but their hearts are far from me. They worship me in vain; their teachings are but rules taught by men.'" (Mark 7:6-7)

2) *Your gift or talent does not supersede your relationship.*

For years, I tried to get by on raw talent and yesterday's anointing without really knowing God! As a PK (Preacher's Kid), I grew up in the church, and I always knew the right "church" thing to say. I could deliver a devotional, sing, play instruments, and quote scripture (mostly memory verses). I even knew how to raise my hands and do a little "shout" when required, but I had no real relationship with God. I had all of the form but none of the substance, and everyone let me keep doing it because I was good at it. Yes, I was a first-class imposter! Therefore, I can speak to the need for an authentic relationship with the Father. Believe me, it is not your gift that matters... It's your relationship.

3)   *You cannot lead where you do not go.*

Many want to lead worship in a public place before many people, but they don't experience God's presence outside of Sunday worship. It is important to read and study the Word of God so that you will be strong in your faith and able to adequately minister to others. It is also important to spend time talking to God.

I guess the real question is: "What is your worship lifestyle?" I hope it is not limited to an exclusive showing on Sundays because if that is the case, I need to be the first to tell you that you would not know God's voice if you heard it. He is always speaking fresh rhema (relevant) word to those who spend time with Him. When is the last time you did something "different" or "fresh" in worship?

Whatever you do on Sunday is really not as impressive as what you do Monday through Saturday. Do you lead your children in worship? Is there worship taking place daily in your house, or on your job? Sunday morning should merely be a manifestation of who you are and what you do all week long. In fact, what qualifies you to lead worship publicly is your worship privately. It's your lifestyle of worship.

4)   *Your level of relationship will determine your level of authority..."Authorized Worship."*

Imagine for a moment, going to my bank and trying to withdraw some money from my account, and you don't know me (or at least, we haven't been in relationship for quite some time!!).

The bank will pull the signature card, ask for your identification, determine you are not who you claim to be, and deny you access to my account. You might be arrested! Why? Because you are fraudulently trying to gain access to something that you have no right to. Could it be that sometimes we operate this way during worship by fraudulently trying to access and activate the presence of God without authorization? We must understand that it takes a relationship to get authority to access benefits. If there is no relationship in place, there is no access to the blessing and benefits of power that having a relationship brings to the worshipper.

5) *You must worship with your heart not your head.*
Intellectual Worship vs. Experiential Worship.

Intellectual worship is empty of power and effectiveness. For example, I intellectually understand the effects drugs can have on a person's life because I have read literature, watched media reports, and conducted interviews. I believe I could convincingly articulate how harmful drugs are and what they can do in a negative sense to a person's life and body. However, when I persuade someone that drugs are a bad decision, I can only do it from an intellectual standpoint because I have never had first hand experience with the devastation of drug addiction.

Now stop for a moment and consider how powerful, effective, and relevant the same message is when it comes from someone who has had those experiences and lived through them to share them with others. A person who has felt the pain and despair of drug addiction can identify with the emotional and physical scars, the pain of losing everything, rehabilitation stints, and even possible jail time. A person who hascome through by the awesome power of God and has been set free from that addiction can powerfully bring a level of persuasion that I never could!

Our worship must be handled the same way. We must be able to worship with intensity because we have lived the worship before trying to convince someone else to partake of it. Who will listen to you if they can't tell whether or not you are doing the same thing you are asking them to do? Don't be naive; people know a genuine act of worship. It is intimate. It can't be hidden.

I heard an old man once say that there are two things that can't be hidden—smoke and love. If there is a fire, you are going to see smoke. That is a fact. In addition, when someone is in love, there is no way to disguise it. If you love God and spend time worshipping Him, that experience will clothe you like a coat or the smile on a newlywed's face. The experience is so engaging that it will be expressed easily without deliberation. Don't just sing the song, become the song!

6)   *Using the Name In Vain...*

Have you ever met people who "name-drop"? They try to make others think they know someone or are related to someone well-known in an effort to make themselves look important. In the final analysis, the people whose names they mention usually don't even know who they are. If you are not careful, you could sometimes be like that.

What we tend to do is use God's name frequently while praying, leading worship, or giving someone a "word"(Matt. 6:5) and conveniently when it suits us. However, may I ask a question of you? Does God even know who you are? I ask this question, not from the standpoint of God knowing you from a Creator to creation standpoint, but from a worshipper to Almighty God stance.

For instance, what if someone you didn't know was convicted of a crime, and when it came time to speak to the judge,he gave you all the credit for inspiring him to commit the crime! That sounds like the ranting of a mad man or woman. On top of that, you would be furious! What nerve they have saying your name. You don't even know them in any intimate way. What a mess! How do you think God identifies with your using His name when He has had no contact with you?

7)   *Are you really in the right place? Qualified/Called/*
      Prepared.

There must be a concrete mechanism in place to evaluate a person's "calling" to a particular area of ministry. When this process of evaluation is neglected, it wreaks havoc on the proper function of ministry. The fact is that a place where this mechanism is not enforced is a haven for ministry imposters. There are no checks and balances, so they roam the church being ineffective and bringing disruption to the flow of ministry.

Just think, have you ever been led in worship by a mean worship leader? Did this person obviously seem far better suited for security than leading worship? Imposter. Do you have someone on your team who quits regularly? Guess what? Imposter. Can you identify someone who will not attend choir rehearsals because he feels his talent will get him through? Imposter. We can all identify someone who really should have never become a part of the choir in the first place because his gifting is not in that area. You guessed it! Imposter.

It is important to note again here that just because a person is a great singer does not necessarily translate into her being a great worship leader. There is a unique anointing/gifting for that which must be evident in a person that is called to be a worship leader. This applies to choir members as well. Just because a person has a great voice does not mean he or she is suited for the discipline it takes to be part of a cohesive group like the choir.

It's not about the performance; it's about HIS presence. If I could be a wind up doll that has one word to say on this subject, it would be "calling, calling, calling." Are you called to lead worship? Are you called to be in the choir? These are simple questions to answer.

"But the hour cometh, and now is, when the true worshippers shall worship the Father in spirit and in truth: for the Father seeketh such to worship

him. God is a Spirit: and they that worship him must worship him in spirit and in truth."

(John 4:23-24)

Imposters must be told the truth in love. "Speaking the truth in love." (Eph. 4:15.) They must be repositioned in the ministry because they will be successful only in the area in which they are "called" to operate. If they are allowed to continue in their deception, it hurts all of us in the long run. Why? Because there is a blockage in the heart, which causes us not to flow as smoothly and effectively as we should. If the heart is not operating at its full capacity, it is not able to clean out any other contaminates that enter the body.

8)   *Your feelings will fool you.*

The presence of God is the motivation for what you do as a Christian. Your commitment is not such that you simply say I am a Christian and live something totally different. The same holds true when you enter the house of the Lord.

Music ministry is not about the ritualistic banter we generally promote as worship. It's not about how loud you scream, how much you shout, how well you sing, or how high your hands are raised. And it is most certainly not about the praise and acceptance from other people. What matters most is our relationship with God. Therein, again lies the true essence of worship. It's not about a "feeling"; it's always about His presence.

The manifestation of His presence may be different from one Sunday to the next, but if you get caught up in a certain feeling you had last week, you may actually miss what God is doing for you today.

Generally speaking, how you feel is really irrelevant to leading worship. It is unfair to project your feelings and attitudes onto the congregation. If you call 911 for help because your house is on fire, you don't want to hear the 911 operator tell you how her day is going or what emergency situations have occurred in her life. At that moment, she becomes irrelevant; you simply want help for your situation, and you want it NOW!

This is the same comprehension of the congregation that must be clear to you as well. Many of these people are in desperate life situations. They are broken and hurting and they are not interested in how you feel. They just want to be ushered into the presence of God. We must look past ourselves and help them get to the place from which their help is coming…. the Lord.

"My help cometh from the LORD, which made heaven and earth."
(Psalms 121:2)

9)   *True worship leaders are a rare breed with many battle scars!*

Another tell-tale sign of an imposter is his systematic, deliberate avoidance of challenges, and or difficulties. Imposters want the benefits of their position, but once they sense the first sign of confrontation or a negative situation arising, they refuse to hold on to their "God-given Call."

A true worshipper understands that relationship is not always easy. In fact, a sincere worshipper understands that what he does will many times be devoid of any praise or recognition, and he may experience some level of loneliness and isolation. At time, he could feel like running off the platform in tears because of the disheartening encounters with people.

Although all these things may be true, the worshipper understands that he has been called to the frontline and is determined and committed to carrying out the mandate that God has placed on his life. He realizes that he will experience setbacks, isolation, and a few battle scars. "*….they are the kind of worshippers the Father seeks*" (John 4:23).

A sincere, committed worshipper is a rare breed. He or

she generally seeks to be invisible. He is not looking for attention, but derives satisfaction when the Father can be seen through his expression of worship. A worship leader who seeks to make him/herself invisible is saying, " Don't focus on me; worship Him with me." Their heart's desire is that there is nothing to distract others from seeing the glory of God manifested in worship. If possible, this worshipper would lead worship behind a draped curtain if they could, because their heart is focused on bringing the sweet fragrance of worship to the heavens and not on becoming the next poster child of praise.

10)   *Developing a strong relationship is a daily natural and spritual process.*

We have touched on the need for a relationship a few times previously. It is important to place a premium on relationships that are dear to you. If you go any length of time without talking to, or spending time with, someone with whom you are in relationship—a spouse, mother or father, brother or sister, or a close friend, you will soon find that your relationship has become strained to say the least. Why? Because if you go long enough, you will find that the two of you no longer know each other. There will be distance and severe damage to the relationship. The fact is you and I must constantly grow in and work on our relationships.

Those who are in an intimate relationship with someone know first hand that the work didn't stop when you agreed to be in a relationship or even after a few phone conversations. The work, in fact, was just beginning. It takes continuous effort to keep that relationship healthy and whole. One of the benefits of a healthy thriving relationship is the level of emotional intimacy that can be shared between the two people. But in order to secure this kind of emotional trust, there must be relationship. One does not come before the other.

The same is true with God. Relationship and worship have a unique language. Because God is a Spirit, one of the ways He communicates with you and you with Him is through your spirit. Therefore, you must understand spiritual things. So speaking and understanding the same language is imperative if you are going to develop a relationship with the Father. Let us say for instance, you travel to Russia but you cannot speak the language. It goes without saying that you are going to have some problems with communication. And, if you cannot communicate with them, how are you going to get to know them?

It is a pleasure to get to know the Father. He has deep, intimate things He wants to share with you, but He will not share those things with strangers. Would you share your deepest, most personal secrets with someone you do not know? Absolutely not. Why? Because if you don't know them, you are not sure what their motivation is or if they truly have your best interest at heart; simply stated, you don't know if you can trust them. It is only after investing the time necessary to develop a solid relationship with someone and really getting to know them that you feel comfortable enough to share your heart with him or her. This is the basic premise of any relationship. God is the one who developed this principle of relational function, so it would stand to reason that He Himself would operate within the context He desires for you to operate in. He is your example, and as a father, He is always teaching you His way of handling yourself. In this instance, He is teaching us that there is no intimacy between strangers.

The core of my heart is that God's people function in the place that God designed for them to function. I know we all have many talents and abilities. I have a friend who can do many things very well, but I am constantly telling him that being in the proper place is what is most important. The question you must answer is what were you made to do? Don't assume because you can imitate the external functions of something that it magically turns you into what you are imitating. If you stand in a garage and make "beep, beep" noises, it does not make you a car. A car has its own unique internal characteristics and qualities. There is substantial time and effort that goes into making sure the car functions according to the specifications of the designer. You know it is a car because of the uniquely specific basic functions cars were designed to perform.

The worship leader, musician, choir member, or sound person is no different. Remember, everything we do—good or bad—is a reflection of our relationship with the Father. "God is spirit, and his worshipers **must** worship in spirit and in truth." The word 'must' leaves you no room for optional compliance. Must means not optional, no choice, has to, required to, no other way. Any other offer of worship is artificial, hollow, empty, and untrue. It is only out of a healthy, pure, and true relationship with God, that healthy, fresh, vibrant, and truly relevant worship comes.

Throughout the pages of this book, we have considered many things with regard to the development and growth of music ministry. There is much work to be done, and it will take determination and courage to continue to seek God concerning His plan for your particular ministry situation. As I have said consistently, "calling" is important. Make up your mind to discover what yours is. Seek God, and once you discover your place, don't be afraid to step down if you realize that you are not where you should be. You will only flourish if you do whatever you must do to fulfill the purpose God has placed in you. The reality is that many will not realize their full potential as a consequence of not embracing the great power that lies within an intimate relationship with the Father. We began this book on the importance of relationship and are ending it in the same vein. Relationship is the gas that will cause your car to go. Yes, you are gifted. Yes, you are talented. Yes, people always seem to respond favorably to your performance. But, does God know your name? Is there a true relationship? That's what the Father desires most...you!

Your relationship with the object of your worship is the paramount reason for your success. Do what you must, but don't neglect to refocus and reestablish your purpose for being involved in music ministry as a priestly designation. You have been chosen to establish the music ministry on earth. What an awesome assignment! You have been hand picked to emulate the priceless sound in heaven. You are in a special place at the designated time. No one can take your place, but you must arm your heart, making yourself ready to take your music to a level far greater than a simple performance, but to a holy offering of perfect praise!

Music Ministry Scriptural Principles
(Reference Items)

WE WERE CREATED TO PRAISE GOD

Isaiah 43:21
This people have I formed for myself; they shall shew forth my praise.(KJV)

Psalm 102:18
This shall be written for the generation to come: and the people which shall be created shall praise the LORD. (KJV).

1 Peter 2:9
But ye are a chosen generation, a royal priesthood, an holy nation, a peculiar people; that ye should shew forth the praises of him who hath called you out of darkness into his marvellous light: (KJV)

Revelation 4:11
Thou art worthy, O Lord, to receive glory and honour and power: for thou hast created all things, and for thy pleasure they are and were created.(KJV)

THERE IS POWER IN ANOINTED MUSIC

1 Samuel 16:14-23
But the Spirit of the LORD departed from Saul, and an evil spirit from the LORD troubled him. And Saul's servants said unto him, Behold now, an evil spirit from God troubleth thee. Let our lord now command thy servants, which are before thee, to seek out a man, who is a cunning player on an harp: and it shall come to pass, when the evil spirit from God is on thee, that he shall play with his hand, and thou shalt be well. And Saul said unto his servants, Provide me now a man that can play well, and bring him to me. Then answered one of the servants, and said, Behold, I have seen a son of Jesse the Bethlehemite, that is cunning in playing, and a mighty valiant man, and a man of war, and prudent in matters, and a comely person, and the LORD is with him. Wherefore Saul sent messengers unto Jesse, and said, Send me David thy son, which is with the sheep. And Jesse took an ass laden with bread, and a bottle of wine, and a kid, and sent them by David his son unto Saul. And David came to Saul, and stood before him: and he loved him greatly; and he became his armourbearer.

And Saul sent to Jesse, saying, Let David, I pray thee, stand before me; for he hath found favour in my sight. And it came to pass, when the evil spirit from God was upon Saul, that David took an harp, and played with his hand: so Saul was refreshed, and was well, and the evil spirit departed from him. (KJV)

2 Kings 3:11-17

But Jehoshaphat said, Is there not here a prophet of the LORD, that we may inquire of the LORD by him? And one of the king of Israel's servants answered and said, Here is Elisha the son of Shaphat, which poured water on the hands of Elijah. And Jehoshaphat said, The word of the LORD is with him. The king of Israel and Jehoshaphat and the king of Edom went down tohim. And Elisha said unto the king of Israel, What have I to do with thee? get thee to the prophets of thy father, and to the prophets of thy mother. And the king of Israel said unto him, Nay: for the LORD hath called these three kings together, to deliver them into the hand of Moab. And Elisha said, As the LORD of hosts liveth, before whom I stand, surely, were it not that I regard the presence of Jehoshaphat the king of Judah, I would not look toward thee, nor see thee. But now bring me a minstrel. And it came to pass, when the minstrel played, that the hand of the LORD came upon him. And he said, Thus saith the LORD, Make this valley full of ditches. For thus saith the LORD, Ye shall not see wind, neither shall ye see rain; yet that valley shall be filled with water, that ye may drink, both ye, and your cattle, and your beasts. (KJV)

2 Chronicles 20:20-25

And they rose early in the morning, and went forth into the wilderness of Tekoa: and as they went forth, Jehoshaphat stood and said, Hear me, O Judah, and ye inhabitants of Jerusalem; Believe in the LORD your God, so shall ye be established; believe his prophets, so shall ye prosper. And when he had consulted with the people, he appointed singers unto the LORD, and that should praise the beauty of holiness, as they went out before the army, and to say, Praise the LORD; for his mercy endureth for ever. And when they began to sing and to praise, the LORD set ambushments against the children of Ammon, Moab, and amount Seir, which were come against Judah; and they were smitten. For the children of Ammon and Moab stood up against the inhabitants of mount Seir, utterly to slay and destroy them: and when they had made an end of the inhabitants of Seir, every one helped to destroy another. And when Judah came toward the watch tower in the wilderness, they looked unto the multitude, and, behold, they were dead bodies fallen to the earth, and none escaped. And when Jehoshaphat and his people came to take away the spoil of them, they found among them in abundance both riches with the dead bodies, and precious jewels, which they stripped off for themselves, more than they could carry away: and they were three days in gathering of the spoil, it was so much. (KJV)

SATAN' MAKE UP & INFLUENCE IN MUSIC

Ezekiel 28:13-15

Thou hast been in Eden the garden of God; every precious stone was thy covering, the sardius, topaz, and the diamond, the beryl, the onyx, and the jasper, the sapphire, the emerald, and the carbuncle, and gold: the workmanship of thy tabrets and of thy pipes was prepared in thee in the day that thou wast created. Thou art the anointed cherub that covereth; and I have set thee so: thou wast upon the holy mountain of God; thou hast walked up and down in the midst of the stones of fire. Thou wast perfect in thy ways from the day that thou wast created, till iniquity was found in thee. (KJV)

Isaiah 14:11-17

Thy pomp is brought down to the grave, and the noise of thy viols: the worm is spread under thee, and the worms cover thee. How art thou fallen from heaven, O Lucifer, son of the morning! how art thou cut down to the ground, which didst weaken the nations! For thou hast said in thine heart, I will ascend into heaven, I will exalt my throne above the stars of God: I will sit also upon the mount of the congregation, in the sides of the north:I will ascend above the heights of the clouds; I will be like the most High. Yet thou shalt be brought down to hell, to the sides of the pit. They that see thee shall narrowly look upon thee, and consider thee, saying, Is this the man that made the earth to tremble, that did shake kingdoms; That made the world as a wilderness, and destroyed the cities thereof; that opened not the house of his prisoners?(KJV)

GOD DOES NOT HONOR UNCLEAN PRAISE

Amos 5:21-24

I hate, I despise your feast days, and I will not smell in your solemn assemblies. Though ye offer me burnt offerings and your meat offerings, I will not accept them: neither will I regard the peace offerings of your fat beasts. Take thou away from me the noise of thy songs; for I will not hear the melody of thy viols. But let judgment run down as waters, and righteousness as a mighty stream. (KJV)

Amos 6:3-5

Ye that put far away the evil day, and cause the seat of violence to come near; That lie upon beds of ivory, and stretch themselves upon their couches, and eat the lambs out of the flock, and the calves out of the midst of the stall; That chant to the sound of the viol, and invent to themselves instruments of musick, like David; (KJV)

Proverbs 15:8

The sacrifice of the wicked is an abomination to the LORD: but the prayer of the upright is his delight. KJV

Isaiah 1:11-18

To what purpose is the multitude of your sacrifices unto me? saith the LORD: I am full of the burnt offerings of rams, and the fat of fed beasts; and I delight not in the blood of bullocks, or of lambs, or of he goats. When ye come to appear before me, who hath required this at your hand, to tread my courts? Bring no more vain oblations; incense is an abomination unto me; the new moons and sabbaths, the calling of assemblies, I cannot away with; it is iniquity, even the solemn meeting. Your new moons and your appointed feasts my soul hateth: they are a trouble unto me; I am weary to bear them. And when ye spread forth your hands, I willhide mine eyes from you: yea, when ye make many prayers, I will not hear: your hands are fullof blood. Wash you, make you clean; put away the evil of your doings from before mine eyes; cease to do evil; Learn to do well; seek judgment, relieve the oppressed,judge the fatherless, plead for the widow. Come now, and let us reason together, saith the LORD: though your sins be as scarlet, they shall be as white as snow; though they be red like crimson, they shall be as wool. (KJV)

Isaiah 59:1-2

Behold, the LORD's hand is not shortened, that it cannot have; neither his ear heavy, that it cannot hear: But your iniquities have separated between you and your God, and your sins have hid his face from you, that he will not hear.(KJV)

Genesis 4:3-5

And in process of time it came to pass, that Cain brought of the fruit of the ground an offering unto the LORD. And Abel, he also brought of the firstlings of his flock and of the fat thereof. And the LORD had respect unto Abel and to his offering: But unto Cain and to his offering he had not respect. And Cain was very wroth, and his countenance fell. (KJV)

PROPHECIES WERE SUNG:

Habakkuk 3:17 - 19

Although the fig tree shall not blossom, neither shall fruit be in the vines; the labour of the olive shall fail, and the fields shall yield no meat; the flock shall be cut off from the fold, and there shall be no herd in the stalls: Yet I will rejoice in the LORD, I will joy in the God of my salvation.   The LORD God is my strength, and he will make my feet like hinds' feet, and he will make me to walk upon mine high places. To the chief singer on my stringed instruments. (KJV)

YOU MUST BE A WORSHIPPER

John 4:23

But the hour cometh, and now is, when the true worshippers shall worship the Father in spirit and in truth: for the Father seeketh such to worship him.(KJV)

CAN'T CROSSOVER WITHOUT THE CROSS

1 Corinthians 14:7-8

And even things without life giving sound, whether pipe or harp, except they give a distinction in the sounds, how shall it be known what is piped or harped? For if the trumpet give an uncertain sound, who shall prepare himself to the battle? (KJV)

John 12:32

And I, if I be lifted up from the earth, will draw all men unto me. (KJV)

WHAT IS THE OBJECT OF YOUR WORSHIP?

Exodus 34:14

Do not worship any other god, for the LORD, whose name is jealous, is a jealous God. (NIV)

Deut 8:19-20

And it shall be, if thou do at all forget the LORD thy God, and walk after other gods, and serve them, and worship them, I testify against you this day that ye shall surely perish. As the nations which the LORD destroyeth before your face, so shall ye perish; because ye would not be obedient unto the voice of the LORD your God. (KJV)

Deut 11:16-17

Take heed to yourselves, that your heart be not deceived, and ye turn aside, and serve other gods, and worship them; And then the LORD's wrath be kindled against you, and he shut up the heaven, that there be no rain, and that the land yield not her fruit; and lest ye perish quickly from off the good land which the LORD giveth you.(KJV)

Deut 30:17-20

But if your heart turns away and you are not obedient, and if you are drawn away to bow down to other gods and worship them, I declare to you this day that you will certainly be destroyed. You will not live long in the land you are crossing the Jordan to enter and possess. This day I call heaven and earth as witnesses againstyou that I have set before you life and death, blessings and curses. Now choose life, so that you and your children may live and that you may love the LORD your God, listen to his voice, and hold fast to him. For the LORD is your life, and he will give you many years in the land he swore to give to your fathers, Abraham, Isaac and Jacob. (NIV)

2 Kings 17:36

But the LORD, who brought you up out of the land of Egypt with great power and a stretched out arm, him shall ye fear, and him shall ye worship, and to him shall ye do sacrifice.(KJV)

Ps 81:9-10

There shall no strange god be in thee; neither shalt thou worship any strange god. I am the LORD thy God, which brought thee out of the land of Egypt: open thy mouth wide, and I will fill it.(KJV)

Isaiah 2:8

Their land also is full of idols; they worship the work of their own hands, that which their own fingers have made: (KJV)

Jeremiah 7:2

Stand in the gate of the LORD's house, and proclaim there this word, and say, Hear the word of the LORD, all ye of Judah, that enter in at these gates to worship the LORD.(KJV)

Matthew 4:10

Then saith Jesus unto him, Get thee hence, Satan: for it is written, Thou shalt worship the Lord thy God, and him only shalt thou serve. (KJV)

Matthew 15:9

But in vain they do worship me, teaching for doctrines the commandments of men.(KJV)

Mark 7:7

Howbeit in vain do they worship me, teaching for doctines the commandments of men.(KJV)

Luke 4:7-8

If thou therefore wilt worship me, all shall be thine. And Jesus answered and said unto him, Get thee behind me, Satan: for it is written, Thou shalt worship the Lord thy God, and him only shalt thou serve.(KJV)

Acts 17:22-30

Paul then stood up in the meeting of the Areopagus and said: "Men of Athens! I see that in every way you are very religious. For as I walked around and looked carefully at your objects of worship, I even found an altar with this inscription: TO AN UN-KNOWN GOD. Now what you worship as something unknown I am going to proclaim to you. "The God who made the world and everything in it is the Lord of heaven and earth and does not live in temples built by hands. And he is not served by human hands, as if he needed anything, because he himself gives all men life and breath and everything else. From one man he made every nation of men, that they should inhabit the whole earth; and he determined the times set for them and the exact places where they should live. God did this so that men would seek him and per-haps reach   out for him and find him, though he is not far from each one of us. 'For in him we live and move and have our being.' As some of your own poets have said, 'We are his offspring.'" Therefore since we are God's offspring, we should not think that the divine being is like gold or silver or stone-an image made by man's design and skill. In the past God overlooked such igno-rance, but now he commands all people everywhere to repent. (NIV)

Isaiah 42:8

I am the LORD: that is my name: and my glory will I not give to another, neither my praise to graven images. (KJV)

Isaiah 48:11

For my own sake, for my own sake, I do this.How can I let myself be defamed? I will not yield my glory to another. (NIV)

Isaiah 44:6

Thus saith the LORD the King of Israel, and his redeemer the LORD of hosts; I am the first, and I am the last; and beside me there is no God.(KJV)

Acts 10:25-26

And as Peter was coming in, Cornelius met him, and fell down at his feet, and worshipped him. But Peter took him up, saying, Stand up; I myself also am a man.(KJV)

FROM THE VERY BEGINNING CREATION SINGS/WORSHIPS

Job 38:7

When the morning stars sang together, and all the sons of God shouted for joy? (KJV)

Psalm 65:13

The pastures are clothed with flocks; the valleys also are covered over with corn; they shout for joy, they also sing. (KJV)

Isaiah 49:13

Sing, O heavens; and be joyful, O earth; and break forth into singing, O mountains: for the LORD hath comforted his people, and will have mercy upon his afflicted. (KJV)

Isaiah 55:12

For ye shall go out with joy, and be led forth with peace: the mountains and the hills shall break forth before you into singing, and all the trees of the field shall clap their hands. (KJV)

Psalm 98:8

Let the floods clap their hands: let the hills be joyful together. (KJV)

Isaiah 52:9

Break forth into joy, sing together, ye waste places of Jerusalem: for the LORD hath comforted his people, he hath redeemed Jerusalem.(KJV).

Psalm 104:12

By them shall the fowls of the heaven have their habitation, which sing among the branches.(KJV)

Luke 19:40

And he answered and said unto them, I tell you that, if these should hold their peace, the stones would immediately cry out. (KJV)

EVERYONE IS COMMANDED TO DO SO

<u>Psalm 145:21</u>

My mouth shall speak the praise of the LORD: and let all flesh bless his holy name for ever and ever. (KJV)

<u>Psalm 66:4</u>

All the earth shall worship thee, and shall sing unto thee; they shall sing to thy name. Selah. (KJV)

Below is a list of Music Theory Defintions to aid in concept development and execution.

A CAPPELLA
Without instrumental accompaniment
CHOIR
An organized company of singers, especially in church service.
COVER
Remake of a song
CRESCENDO
A gradual increase in volume.
CROSSOVER MUSIC
Music that is played in a variety of formats/styles
DECRESCENDO
A gradual decrease in volume.
DYNAMICS
Variation in intensity of musical sound.
GENRE
A kind; sort; type
GOSPEL
Good News; of or pertaining to the teaching of Jesus Christ; Contemporary living or happening in the same period of time;
HARMONY
The simulations comb notes in a chord.
INVERSION
Vocally speaking, changing or flipping the position of the vocal chord/parts (Sop.,Alto,Ten), up or down within the same key.
MODULATION
The process of changing from one key to another within a composition.
MUSIC
From the Greek word: Sumphonia; the art of combining sounds or sequences of notes into harmonious patterns pleasing to the ear and satisfying to the emotions.
MUSICIANSHIP
Skill, insight, and artistry in the performance of music.

OCTAVE
The eighth note above a given pitch.
PITCH
To set in a particular key (tone on a scale).
RHYTHM
The term which denotes the organization of sound in time; the temporal quality of sound.
SECULAR
Of or belonging to the world or worldly things as distinguished from the church and religious affairs; not sacred or religious; temporal.
STYLE
Distinction, excellence, originality and character in any form of artistic or literally expression.
TEMPO
The rate of speed of a musical work.
TIMBRE
The quality of sound that distinguishes it from other sounds of the same pitch and volume.
TONE
Musical note; characteristics quality of a particular instrument or voice.
UNISON
Singing or playing the same notes by all singers or players, either at exactly the same pitch or in a different octave.
VIBRATO
A slightly tremulous effect imparted to vocal or instrumental tone, for warmth and color.
VOICE
Musical sound produced by the vocal chords and resonated by the cavities of the head and throat.

BIBLIOGRAPHY

Alderson, Richard. Complete Handbook of Voice Training. Tenth ed. West Nyack, NY: Parker Publishing Company, Inc. 1988.

Burroughs, Bob. An ABC Primer for Church Musicians. Nashville, Tennessee: Broadman Press. 1990

Hibbert, Mike and Viv. Music Ministry. Christchurch, New Zealand: Mike and Viv Hibbert. 1982.

Lester, Lilly. The Prayer Habit. Nashville, Tennessee: Serenity Publishing & Communications, Inc. 2003.

Roget's II The New Thesaurus. Boston, Mass.: Houghton Mifflin Company. 1988.

Strong, James. The New Strong's Exhaustive Concordance of the Bible. Nashville, Tennessee: Thomas Nelson Publishers. 1984.

The American Heritage Dictionary. 3rd ed. New York: Dell Publishing. 1994.

Unger, Merrill F. The New Unger's Bible Dictionary. Chicago, Illinois: Moody Press. 1988.

Webster's New World Dictionary and Thesaurus. New York: Simon and Schuster, Inc. 1996.

About the Author

JOE PACE

A Grammy, Dove, and Stellar nominated songwriter, producer, artist, director and author, Joseph W. Pace, II is a multi-talented and gifted man with a wide range of abilities and insight in the realm of gospel music ministry. His anointed style, production, spiritual perception, and song writing skills have established him as one of the gospel music industry's most dynamic and compelling talents.

An ordained minister, Joe Pace also wears many other hats. In addition to being the Director/CEO of the award-winning Colorado Mass Choir, he is also the owner and president of Pace Productions, Inc., a gospel music production, publishing and management company. Minister Pace's gift has allowed him to minister to a multitude of different audiences throughout the United States and abroad. However, his first consideration has always been to ministry at the local level. To that end, he has served in the capacity of Minister of Music/Music Pastor for both small and large ministries across the country. Pace is also a frequent writer/columnist for many top Christian music publications.

While working as an artist, producer, and songwriter for Integrity Gospel, Pace created a line of praise and worship music resources for the church. The "Joe Pace Presents" product line includes the double Dove Award nominated album, Joe Pace Presents... *Let There Be Praise,* the Top 10 Billboard Charting project *Joe Pace Presents... Shake The Foundation, The Best Of Joe Pace Songbook,* and *Joe Pace Presents... Sunday Morning Service.* All have won critical acclaim for their technical excellence and their "usability" by local churches.

Pace 's intense scriptural understanding and anointing in the area of music ministry, as well as his over 20 years of experience in music ministry, have rendered him a phenomenal teacher and much sought after workshop clinician. As a leader in the area of cross-cultural worship and an extremely-engaging instructor, he has conducted numerous music workshops throughout the country and is an increasingly requested speaker at major conferences. He also partnered with Integrity Music to be one of their featured instructors in their "Seminars4Worship" national conference series alongside such distinguished Christian leaders as Dr. Jack Hayford, Pastor Pete Sanchez, and Don Moen.

Although he has worked with many renowned gospel artists and is in great demand nationally for his multitude of talents, the spotlight is not something Minister Pace seeks. His ambition is only to continue to produce, write, and teach that which facilitates and enables people to experience Christ on a personal level.

For workshops and speaking engagements or to purchase compact discs and other resources offered by Joe Pace visit him on-line at:

www.joepace.org

www.performancetoprasie.com

Sunday Morning Service

Let There Be Praise

Glad About It

Shake the Foundation

Speak Life

You can write the author at:
Serenity Publishing & Communications, Inc.
P.O. Box 282282
Nashville, TN 37228
www.serenitypc.com

Printed in the United States
21225LVS00007B/1-99

9 780971 270183